# The MG Collection

Patrick Stephens Limited, an imprint of Haynes Publishing, has published authoritative, quality books for enthusiasts for more than 25 years. During that time the company has established a reputation as one of the world's leading publishers of books on aviation, maritime, military, model-making, motor cycling, motoring, motor racing, railway and railway modelling subjects. Readers or authors with suggestions for books they would like to see published are invited to write to: The Editorial Director, Patrick Stephens Limited, Sparkford, Nr Yeovil, Somerset, BA22 7JJ.

# The MG Collection

## THE PRE-WAR MODELS

# RICHARD MONK

### Foreword by Rivers Fletcher

Patrick Stephens Limited

First published 1994 by Patrick Stephens Limited
in association with the MG Owners' Club.

Reprinted 1996

The MG badge and octagon are registered
trade marks and are used by kind permission
of the Rover Group.

British Library Cataloguing-in-Publication Data:
A catalogue record for this book
is available from the British Library

ISBN 1 85260 496 4

Patrick Stephens Limited is an imprint of
Haynes Publishing, Sparkford,
Nr Yeovil, Somerset, BA22 7JJ

Designed and typeset by Kelvin Blyth Studios, Swavesey, Cambridge
Printed in Italy by G. Canale & C. S.p.A. – Borgaro Torinese (Turin)

# Contents

# Foreword

What a very good idea to make a book of Richard Monk's photographic collection of the pre-war MGs. In Mike Allison's first edition of *The Magic of MG* we already have those cars well listed and illustrated, but with Richard's collection we now have a great deal more information and absolutely splendid colour photographs. Richard concentrates on the standard production models but adds many of the best known special editions produced by coachbuilders of that time. The early bullnosed and flat radiator models are covered and most of the 18/80s and 18/100 have been photographed well and in restored condition. All these cars mean so much to me because I knew them and drove them when they were new.

The decision to illustrate all the pre-war models in new or even better than new condition is excellent and again it pleases me greatly because, of course, I knew those cars in that perfect condition. Some people prefer to see old cars looking well used, in original paintwork and trim, and they have a point in respect of originality which has now become such a fetish, but I think that Richard was right - this fine collection represents the cars as they would have been in their day.

There are splendid examples of the early Midgets and now there are queries with regard to that difficult word 'replica'. A replica Double Twelve is well described and illustrated and this is correct because that model was a catalogued production car. The original Double Twelve MG, such as WL 9273 which I share with Elizabeth Wigg, was not available to the public and only five were produced for the Double Twelve race at Brooklands in 1930. There are really excellent photographs of the F Type Magna collection, such an important series starting with the small six-cylinder cars which led to the Magnettes which dominated such a lot of racing in the 1930s.

I am particularly glad that Richard has covered the SA, VA and WA series. Most of the press and many MG enthusiasts criticised the performance of these cars, comparing them with the overhead camshaft MGs which were so successful in competition. But the pushrod overhead valve SA, VA and WA models were built as Sports Tourers, not for racing or tough trials with which most enthusiasts identified MGs. In fact, all these cars had excellent touring performance and happen to be delightful pre-war cars for use on the road today, even motorways!

This collection was of course previously published in *Enjoying MG,* the monthly magazine of the MG Owners' Club. Roche Bentley and Richard Monk have developed the Club into the largest, strongest and most powerful MG organisation. The Club is unique and is very successful because it is run by enthusiasts, rather like the MG Car Company at Abingdon was in the old days.

This book is tremendously valuable for all of us and I look forward to seeing the post-war models covered in the same way in due course.

A. F. Rivers Fletcher

# The MG Collection

## Pre-War Models

OWNERS' CLUB

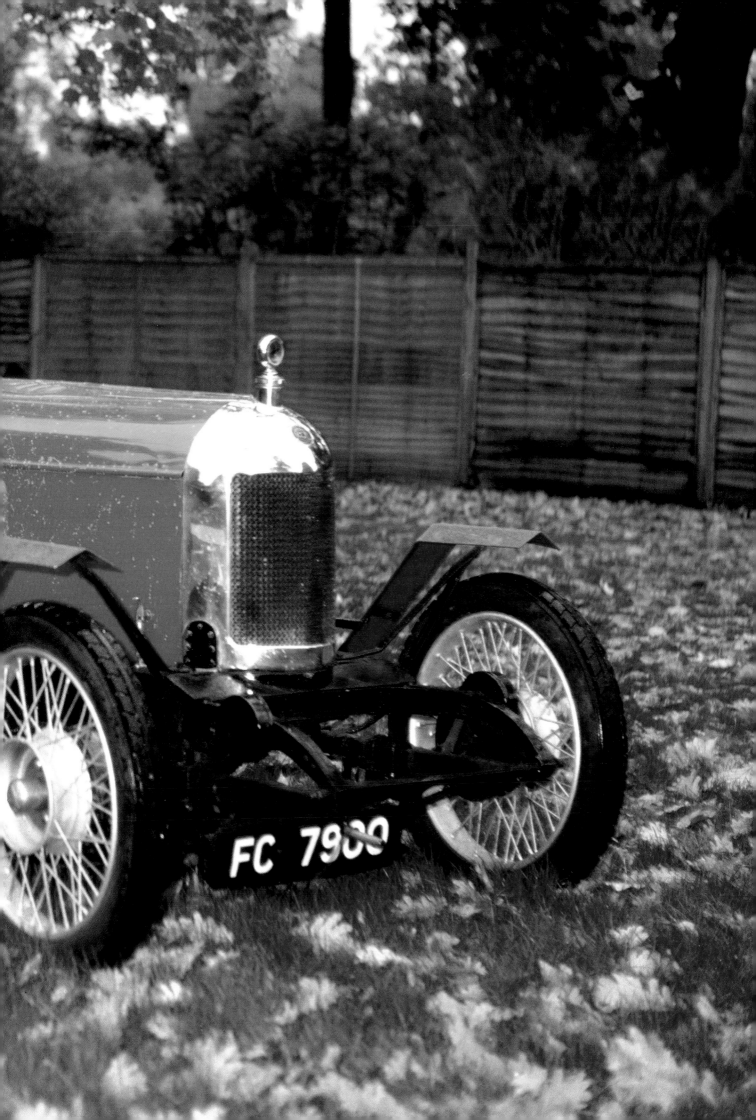

There are differing views amongst Car Historians as to whether Old Number One was the original and first MG built. MGs were built for some two years before Old Number One came on the scene. It is certainly true that this vehicle was the first MG to be built specifically to compete in sporting events.

The first cars known MGs were in fact special bodied Morris Cowleys. Old Number One was first seen at the 1925 Lands End Trial. Cecil Kimber had the car specially built to compete in the trial and this was indeed based on a bullnose Morris Cowley chassis. The rear section was modified, the chassis frame being cut off and having new rails fitted which curved up and over the rear axle to secure splayed rear springs. The engine was a special overhead valve Hotchkiss with a capacity of 1548cc. Tuning amounted to machining and polishing the cylinder head and minor carburation modifications. The 11.9 hp engine was then linked to the standard Morris transmission employing a 3 speed manual gearbox. Fuel was introduced to the SU carburettor by a hand operated air pressure pump located next to the gear lever. The suspension arrangements used a standard half elliptic spring at the front, but with special half elliptic rear springs in place of the normal Morris three quarter elliptic. Tall wire spoke wheels were fitted to the standard hubs by three bolts, braking was standard Morris drum system, both front and rear. The only lighting on the car was by two small sidelights mounted on each side of the scuttle and a single headlight which is not evident on the car today. The normally high Cowley steering column was lowered by raking the column. Extra instrumentation included a tachometer, fuel and oil pressure gauges along with the standard speedometer and ammeter.

The special lightweight body was designed and built by Carbodies of Coventry for Kimber, the final assembly of the car was at the Morris factory in Longwall, Oxford and it was originally registered FMO 842 on 27th March 1925 (a new number FC 7900 was allocated the 1950's). Kimber competed very successfully in the Lands End Trial that year, winning a Gold medal in the Light Car Class. Soon after the Trial the car was sold to a friend of Cecil Kimber's for £300. It was reputed to have only cost £279 to build and is now valued at a figure approaching £250,000....(who says MG's are not an appreciating asset!). Old Number Onea was later spotted being used to haul a big food trailer ofv all things and subsequently discovered in a Manchester scrapyard by an employee of the MG Car Company in 1932 and bought for £15. The car was then taken to the Abingdon factory and restored to be used as a promotion vehicle. The Nuffield Organisation were the first to adopt the title Old Number One when they utilised the car in advertising and publicity material for the MG Car Company and the title has remained ever

since. When the car was restored by the factory the colour was changed from the original grey primer to the colour it is today, cherry red. The car has always featured well in MG publicity material and has been exhibited on numerous occasions at home and also abroad, on one occasion it was shipped to the USA to feature in the 50th anniversary celebrations of MG. The car now forms part of the British Motor Industry Heritage Trust Collection at Gaydon, where it is generally on permanent display. It is kept in full running order and indeed throughout its life many privileged journalists, historians and enthusiasts have been allowed to drive the car to assess the merits of the car that helped fuel the tremendous following that the marque now enjoys worldwide.

## SPECIFICATION

### Engine
Type: 11.9 hp Hotchkiss in-line, water-cooled
No. of cylinders: 4
Bore/stroke mm: 69.5 x 102
Displacement cc: 1548
Valve operation: Overhead pushrod
Sparkplugs per cyl.: 1
Compression ratio: 5 : 1
Induction: 1 SU carburettor, air pressure fuel feed, hand pump
BHP: Approximately 25

### Drive Train
Clutch: Wet cork single driven plate
Transmission: Three-speed manual gearbox

### Chassis
Frame: Modified Morris Cowley, twin side members, cross members
Wheelbase mm: 2591
Track - front mm: 1219
Track - rear mm: 1219
Suspension - front: Half-elliptic springs, beam axle
Suspension - rear: Half-elliptic springs, live axle
Brakes: Morris Oxford drums front and rear
Tyre size: 710 x 90
Wheels: Wire spoke

### Performance
Maximum speed: 129 km/h (80mph)
Acceleration: 0 - 60 mph 20 sec
Number built: 1

# 14/40 Super Sports Two Seater

Many people are of the impression that 'Old Number One' was the first MG to be produced. It is true to say that it was the first MG to be built specifically for sporting purposes, however cars that were identifiable as MGs were on the scene some two years before the famous Number One was built. It is worth a brief insight into the circumstances leading up to the birth of MG as there is much debate as to whether the very early Morris based MGs, were in fact MGs.

Cecil Kimber joined Morris Motors in 1921 after several jobs within the motor industry. His first position was as Sales Manager and very soon he became the General Manager having gained the respect of Morris workforce, he was very quickly able to get the company to flourish and change its direction. Kimber realised that the existing Morris models were not particularly exciting and that there was a definite market for cars with a more sporting appeal. Morris already offered a fairly wide range of body styles on their standard chassis, but Kimber set about designing and drawing new bodies that could be fitted easily to the existing chassis. His first offerings were produced in 1922, utilising the chassis and running gear from the cheaper of the bullnosed Morris cars called the Cowley. With special bodywork and lower suspension these cars sold for about the same price as the more fully equipped Morris Oxford. The Chummy as it was called, was an immediate success with over 200 being sold throughout 1922 and 1923. It was effectively an open two seater, with space at the rear for occasional passengers that were also brought in under the canvas hood weather protection, unlike the normal two seater cars that had a Dicky seat arrangement, where the passengers were left to fend for themselves in the elements.

Suddenly the Chummy became obsolete with the introduction by Morris of a virtually identical model known as the Cowley Occasional Four, however Kimber who was an enthusiastic sportsman was keen to enter competitions and he did ·this with success in his own Chummy. He had the car tuned by the factory and in March 1923 he and his co-driver won gold medals in the Lands End Trial. Following

on from this success Kimber decided to introduce a new sporting model. Under Kimbers' direction the Oxford based coachbuilding company, Raworth were engaged to build a neat two seater sports body that was to be fitted to a slightly modified Cowley chassis. With their elegantly curved wings and raked windscreen supported on either side by triangular glass frames, these were decidedly sporting cars. To add to the overall effect a pair of boat type scuttle mounted ventilators were fitted and these features were evident as a hallmark of all subsequent MGs through to 1929. Some consider that the Raworth Sports model was the first true MG, however the radiator was

adorned with a Morris badge but associated advertising carried for the first time the MG stylised letters within the octagon and the car was described as 'The MG Super Sports Morris'. It carried several modifications including flatter road springs, a mildly tuned Hotchkiss engine, bead edged tyres, four wheel braking with servo assistance.

It may not have been until 1925 that MGs went into any volume production and it was at the beginning of 1925 that 'Number One' was built from a combination of various standard and modified Morris components. The engine used was a modified Hotchkiss 11 hp unit and apart from the overhead valve head was the same as that used in the Cowley. Initially the car was reputed to have been finished in dark grey and it was used in various trials by Kimber and others with a measure of success. Despite this success it is likely that Morris did not want to support any further development of what was a solely sporting vehicle and it was sold to one of Kimber's friends. There is no doubt though that

'Number One' had made a significant mark in the MG history books and was a good publicity machine for Kimber. In 1926 attentions were then turned to the extensively modified Morris Oxford 14/28 chassis that were being prepared with MG bodies on them, still with the bull nose Morris radiators the cars were, for their year, extremely attractive and there was a healthy demand for them. Morris Garages cars were now more widely becoming recognised as MGs and it was simply the bull nose radiators that they wore that betrayed the Morris parentage.

At the latter end of 1926, ready for the 1927 model year, Morris decided to adopt some new production techniques learned from the Americans. As a result the bull nose radiator was replaced with a flat fronted type and a wider heavier chassis was adopted to allow much more room inside the cockpit. MGs had no option but to follow suit and potentially the extra weight involved with the chassis was a threat to the performance. However various modifications were made and the Kimber workforce managed to produce an MG version that was equally as fast as its predecessor. Each individual engine was specially tuned and Kimber was able to retain some of the previous elegance of the forerunners to ensure that the body lines were attractive. The heavier chassis did have a plus point in as much as it was more rigid and made the car handle much better with less flexing. During 1927 the engine was considerably uprated to 35 hp and the ride and handling was further improved with flattened springs front and rear and the addition of Hartford shock absorbers. Braking was also modified and the rubber mounted steering replaced by a Marles system. Balloon tyres as opposed to bead edge were now standard together with a quieter exhaust system. On the styling front, engine turned aluminium side panels replaced plain polished aluminium and an attractive two-tone paint system completed the package.

These flat radiator MGs then became known as 14/40s rather than the earlier designation of 14/28 with the 40 coming from an optimistic view of the engine power output. This designation was in common with many other of the major car producers of the time. There is some confusion over the exact configuration of the model sequence but it is generally understood that the first three mark numbers were 14/28s built between 1924 and 1927 and more commonly referred to as simply 'The MG Super Sports' models. The 14/40s were designated Mark IV although to add to the confusion there were some Mark III model 14/28s that appeared with the new flat radiators. The model that superseded the Mark IV at the latter end of 1928, early 1929, did not have a Mark number.

Sales of the MG rose dramatically and in September 1927 an enforced move was made to a new factory in Edmund Road Oxford. Kimber was very pleased with this move and he was quoted as once saying 'this is the only factory of its kind in the world devoted solely to the manufacture of sports cars'. It was at this time that MG became far more independent of Morris Motors, even to the extent of adopting their own chassis number range and the carrying out of all warranty work of cars previously built at the Morris factory. This move to make MG independent of Morris was brought to a logical conclusion when the MG Car Company was established in 1928.

# 14/40

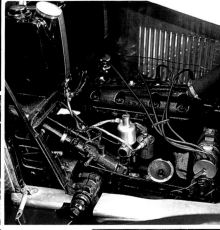
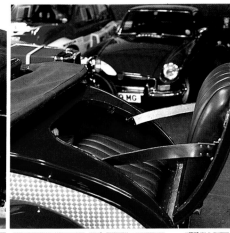

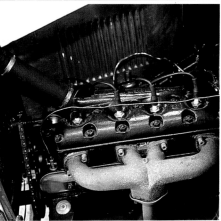

**SPECIFICATION**
Engine
Bore and Stroke: 75mm x 102mm
Capacity: 1802cc
No of cylinders: 4
Valve operation: Side valve with mushroom tappets.
Power output: Approx 35 bhp at 4000 rpm
Drive Train
Clutch: Wet cork
Gearbox: 3 speed non-synchromesh crash box
Brakes: Mechanical, servo assisted until 1928
Drums: 12'' front and rear
Suspension: half elliptic front and rear
Wheels: Bolt-on wire spoke
Wheelbase: 8' 10.5''
Track: 4' 0'' front and rear
Produced: 1926 to late 1929 (includes flat rad 14/28)
Number produced: Approx 900
Price new: 2 seater £340, 4 seater £350, Salonette £475.

# 14/40 Super Sports Four Seater

There are many stories relating to the formative years of MG with many writers and historians each hoping that they have the definitive account of how MG came about. A known fact is that Cecil Kimber was appointed to the position of General Manager of Morris Garages Limited in 1922 having previously been the sales Manager for just over a year. They were the Oxford based distributors for Morris Motors and were owned by William Morris who also owned the production plant in Cowley. Kimber found himself in charge of the day to day administration of a very busy company and it was a tremendous opportunity that he jumped at, particularly as his previous appointments in the motor industry had frustrated him. Within a very short space of time he turned his attentions to developing special bodies for the standard Morris Cowley chassis. There was a call for non-standard cars from customers who did not want the 'run of the mill' item and it was quite usual for some of the larger garages to offer this kind of service with assistance from outside coachbuilders. Kimber was certainly not inspired by the existing range of Morris models and he was well aware that there was a ready market, albeit a small one, for cars with a more sporting appeal.

Morris already offered a fairly wide range of body styles on their standard chassis but Kimber decided that these cars would lend themselves to modification without major expense and he set about designing and drawing new bodies that could be fitted easily to the

existing chassis. His first offerings were produced in 1922 utilising the chassis and running gear from the cheaper of the bullnosed Morris cars, called the Cowley. With modified lower suspension and a raked steering column, the cars sold for about the same price as the more fully equipped Morris Oxford. These cars were more fondly known as "The Chummy" and sported the standard 12 horsepower engine. At the end of the day these cars were still Cowleys in disguise and despite their improved looks did not sell very quickly at first. This was mainly due to the price of £350 which was considered expensive when put alongside the newly introduced Morris "Occasional Four" which was available in 1924 priced at £215.

Kimber started MGs exploits in motor sport when he entered one of his specially tuned Chummys in the 1923 Land's End Trial, winning a gold medal. This achievement did boost sales marginally of the special bodied Morrises whilst Kimber turned his attentions to producing a tuned version of the Chummy on the 14 horsepower Morris Oxford chassis in order to compete with the Occasional Four. Raworth, the Oxford based coachbuilding company were engaged to build a neat two seater sports body that could be fitted to a slightly modified Cowley chassis. With their elegantly curved wings and their raked windscreen, supported on either side by triangular

glass frames, this new model was true sporting machine. To enhance the sporting feel, a pair of boat type ventilators were mounted on top of the scuttle and these were to be a hallmark of subsequent models until 1929. Some consider that the Raworth Sports Model was the first true MG, however the radiator was adorned with a Morris badge and the accompanying advertising literature carried for the first time the stylised MG lettering in the octagon and described the car as "The MG Super Sports Morris". The modifications included flatter road springs, a mildly tuned Hotchkiss engine, bead edge tyres and four wheel braking with servo assistance.

Late in 1924 the renowned "Old Number One" trials car was taking shape in the Longwall Street service depot in Oxford. Kimber had commissioned this car specifically to compete in the 1925 Land's End Trial and it was built up from a combination of various standard and modified Morris components. The engine used was a modified Hotchkiss 11.9 horsepower 1500 cc unit and apart from the overhead valve head was the same as that used in the Cowley. Kimber again secured a gold medal and the resultant publicity gave him the much desired interest in MG. By 1926 attentions were turned to the modified Morris Oxford 14/28 chassis that were being fitted up with MG bodies. They still carried bullnose radiators at this time and were considered a very attractive car which stimulated a healthy demand from the sports-minded car buying public. Morris Garages cars were now becoming more widely recognised as MGs and it was simply the bull nosed radiators that betrayed the Morris parentage. Towards the end of 1926 in readiness for the 1927 model year, Morris decide to adopt some new production techniques imported from the American car industry. As a result the traditional bull nose radiator was replaced with a flat front type and a wider heavier chassis was adopted to give more room for passengers inside the cockpit. Kimber had no option but to follow suit with the MG versions and the extra weight of the chassis was a potential threat to the performance. However various modifications were made by the Kimber workforce with the end result of an MG that was equally as fast as its predecessor. Each engine was finely tuned and during 1927 was considerably uprated to 35 horsepower and with modifica-

tions to the suspension incorporating flattened springs and Hartford shock absorbers, the ride and handling was much improved. Braking efficiency was also enhanced and the rubber mounted steering system was replaced with a Marles Weller arrangement. The bead edged tyres gave way to the balloon variety and a quieter exhaust system completed the mechanical package. On the styling front, engine turned aluminium side panels replaced plain polished aluminium and an attractive two tone paint scheme finished off the car nicely.

The flat radiator MGs were designated 14/40 as opposed to the earlier title 14/28. The '40' came from an optimistic view of the engine power output and was in common with many of the major car producers of the era. There is some confusion over the exact configuration of the model sequence but it is generally understood that the first three mark numbers were 14/28's built between 1924 and 1927 and that they were more commonly referred to as simply "The MG Super Sports" models. The 14/40's were designated Mark IV although to add to the confusion there were some Mark III model 14/28's that appeared with the new flat radiators. The model that superseded the Mark IV at the latter end of 1928 did not have a Mark number allocated. With sales increasing dramatically an enforced move was made in 1927 to a new factory in Edmund Road, Oxford and it was at this time that MG became far more independent of Morris even to the extent of adopting their own chassis number range and the undertaking of all warranty work on MG cars previously built at the Morris factory. This move to give MG its independence was brought to a logical conclusion when the MG Car Company was formed in 1928.

The M.G. Super Sports Two-Seater £340

## The M.G. Two and Four Seaters

BUILT for speed with grace, the M.G. Super Sports models embody all that is best in their category. An amazing acceleration and an immense reserve of power under all circumstances are the features which have won them instant popularity wherever they have been used, and the supreme conduct of their coachwork places them far above others of their class. Their astonishing steadiness on corners is likewise a revolution.

Sole Designers and Producers

# The Morris Garages

Head Office and Showrooms: Queen Street, OXFORD.

## General Specification

The M.G. Super Sports Four-Seater £350

# 14/40 Super Sport 4 Seater

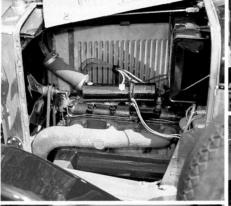

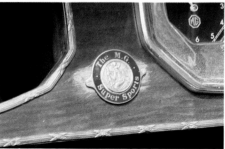

**SPECIFICATION**
Engine:
Bore & Stroke: 75mm x 102mm
Capacity: 1802 cc
No of cylinders: 4 in line
Valve operation: Side valve with mushroom tappets
Power output: Approx 35 bhp at 4,000 rpm
Clutch: Twin plate cork in oil
Gearbox: 3 forward speed crash box
Brakes: Mechanical with servo assistance. 12" drums
Suspension: Half elliptic springs front & rear
Wheels: Bolt on 19" dia wire spoke
Wheelbase: 8' 10.5"
Track: 4' 0" front and rear
Number built: (flat rad) 425

# 18/80 Mk1 Tourer

The MG Six as it was first known was introduced at the 1928 Motor Show and accompanied the 14/40 that was now in its fourth year of production. It was becoming apparent that if public interest was to be maintained in the new MG marque that a new model was needed, hence the launch of the 18/80 model. The significance of the 18/80 was that it was the first 'real' MG simply because the earlier flat radiator and bull nosed cars held such close ties with the Morris equivalents and Cecil Kimber had up until then been charged with upgrading the Morris's to give them a wider appeal. The new 18/80 was a car that could be described as a marque on its own, as the vast majority of the mechanical components were totally different to those of the current Morris.

During 1927 the Morris Light Six was announced which was powered by a two and a half litre, six cylinder engine. An unusual departure for Morris was the fact that the camshaft was above the valves, operating through 'L' shaped rockers. However the car did not reach the production lines and this particular power unit was eventually used in the Morris Major and after that in the Isis. The chassis of the Morris Light Six was not sufficiently rigid enough to cope with stresses imposed by the powerful 60 bhp engine and was redesigned and renamed the Morris Six with little better results. Kimber however saw the potential of this engine for the 18/80 project and Morris Garages purchased a Light Six fabric saloon for evaluation. A brand new chassis frame was made and it was the first time that a chassis unique to MG was produced, all previous ones had been based on the standard Morris chassis. By the time of the 1928 Motor Show, the Light Six engine had been modified with a new block to accommodate twin carburettors that were mounted low down underneath the exhaust manifold with the inlet passing through the block and up to the ports in the head. The cylinder block and crankcase were made in one single casting with a separate cylinder head. A strong 4 main bearing crankshaft was employed with a Duplex chain and gear drive to the camshaft, tensioned by a spring loaded eccentric tensioner. The chain was also utilised to drive the distributor, water pump, oil pump and dynamo all via a single skew gear shaft which occasionally led to running problems. The very latest shell-type big end and main bearings were used which contributed to the very smooth and quiet running of the power unit.

The 18/80 was beautifully constructed with painstaking attention to detail, even the bulkhead support brackets incorporated a fine MG

motif set into the aluminium. Unfortunately these were hidden from view when the bodywork was mounted onto the chassis. Front and rear axles were designed by MG and utilised Perrot type brake gear. Marles steering gear was used and early prototypes had 14/40 type bolt-on wheels, however all the production cars employed Rudge-Whitworth centre-lock wire spoke wheels. The dashboard displayed quality Jaeger instrumentation whilst the steering wheel was adjustable for rake. Behind the dashboard mounted on the engine side of the bulkhead, was a reserve petrol tank and an oil tank of one gallon capacity which fed oil directly into the crankcase. For the first time a fly-off handbrake was used, mounted inboard on the tourer and saloon versions but externally on the speed twin model. Probably the most noticeable feature however was the distinctive new radiator design with the vertical colour-keyed slats and MG Octagon. This basic design of radiator grille was to be used on MGs throughout the years right up to the end of the T series cars.

Upon introduction the basic price of the chassis only was £420 with the buyer then specifying either a tourer or saloon body. The tourer cost a mere £65 extra and the saloon another £135 which by today's standards seems very cheap! The tourer was endowed with a fairly light body compared to the saloon and this allowed pretty brisk acceleration and good top speed compared to the rivals of the day. The MG could easily out accelerate the Lagonda and Alvis models that already held good sporting reputations. In addition to speed the 18/80 had fine responsive steering, excellent roadholding and the three speed gearbox did not prove a drawback due to the good torque characteristics of the engine.

In 1929 a new chassis was designed of much sturdier construction, with a wider track to be designated the Mark II. This was not to replace the Mark I but to sell alongside it and it really must have confused prospective purchasers. The Mark II engaged a track some 4" wider than the Mark I and the already sturdy chassis was heavier than its predecessor. The end result was that the Mark II was considerably slower than the Mark I, especially as there was no increase in power from the same engine. This coupled with the fact that the car was priced at £100 more, made the car difficult to sell. Other improvements were the provision of a four speed gearbox,

uprated cable operated brakes and bodywork of higher standard incorporating wider mudguards. The chassis, although giving greater rigidity and allowing the use of softer road springs, was a penalty against performance. During 1929 the Mark I was improved, being fitted with uprated cable operated brakes and in 1930 a speed model was introduced. A guaranteed 80 mph was claimed for the speed model and a Mark II version was also offered but again suffered with the added weight of the chassis and this detracted from the good acceleration for which the Mark I was admired. Probably the ultimate 18/80 was the Mark III which was an attempt to turn this fine vehicle into a racing car. It was loosely based on the Bentley racing models of the day and constructed on the Mark II 18/80 chassis. The engine was modified and had a cross flow head, the first time one had been used on an MG. A new crankshaft, camshaft and pistons were fitted and dry sump lubrication completed the package. The model became known as the 18/80 'Tigresse' and variously as the 18/100 because of attempts that were never realised to try and produce a 100 bhp and 100 mph motor car. The car certainly looked the part with its outside exhaust ending in the obligatory fishtail, cycle wings, louvred chassis panels and leather bonnet strap, however weight was again a problem penalising the performance. Competition appearances of the car were few and far between with its first outing in the Brooklands Double Twelve 24 hours race in 1930, ending in disaster. The engine seized after running its bearings and to make matters worse, an MG Midget managed to stay the course and finish with a team prize. There was very little public interest shown in the ready-to-race Mark III and only five cars were ever produced, somewhat less than the 25 that Cecil Kimber had hoped for. It was hardly surprising considering the cars carried a £895 price tag. The Mark I stayed in production until early 1931 and the Mark II continued through into 1932. New models were available from stock up until 1934, but sold very slowly. This was a reflection of the depressed state of the world economy rather than on the car itself.

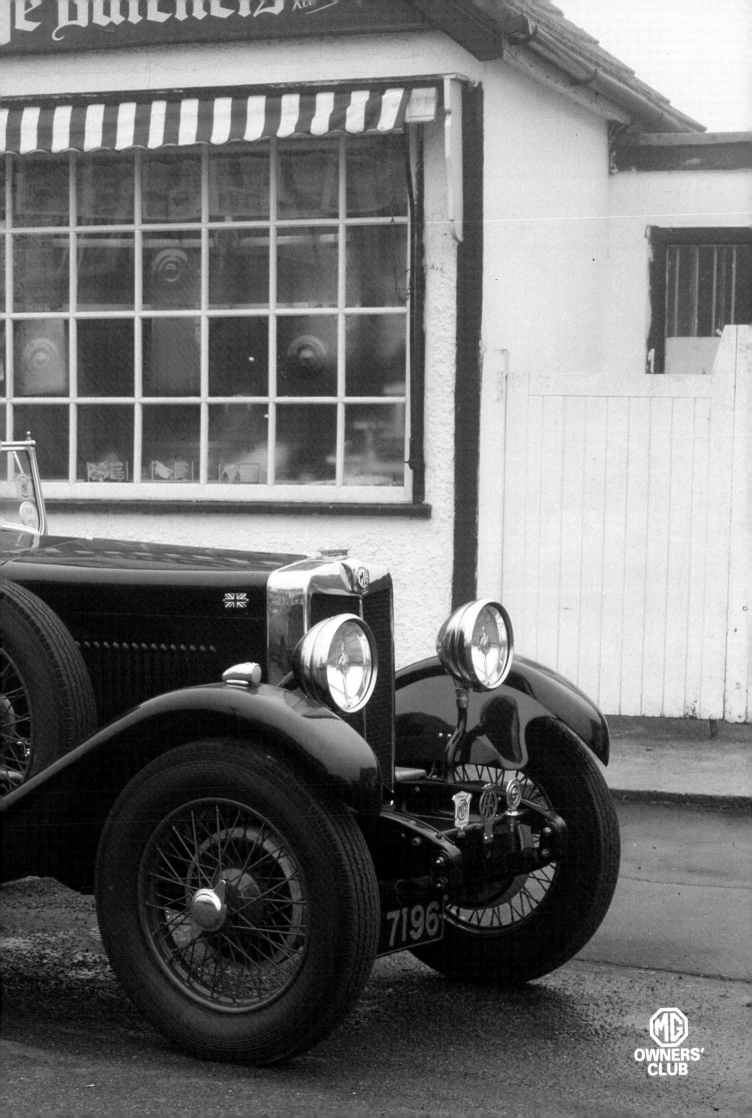

# 18/80 TOURER Mk 1

WL 7196

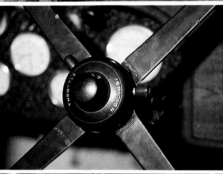

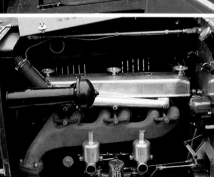

## Specification

**Engine**

Number of cylinders: 6 in ine.

Bore and Stroke: 69mm x 110mm.

Capacity: 2468 cc

Valve operation: Chain driven, single overhead camshaft.

Carburation: Twin horizontal SUs.

Power output: 60 bhp @ 3,200 rpm.

**Drive Train**

Clutch: Double plate, cork inset, automatically lubricated.

Transmission: Manual crash, 3 forward speeds.

Suspension: Semi elliptic front and rear.

Steering: Marles frictionless gear.

Brakes: 12″ drum, Perrot type (early cars). Cable operated (later cars).

Wheels: Centre Lock wire spoke.

Wheelbase: 9″6″

Track: 4′0″

Performance: Max speed; approx 80 mph

MPG; approx 18.

Built: Late 1929 to mid 1933.

# 18/80 Mk1 Twin Door Salonette

The MG 18/80 Sports Six as it was first known was introduced at the 1928 Motor Show and accompanied the 14/40 that was now in its fourth year of production. This was the first time that MGs had appeared in their own right at a motor show and this new car was to satisfy the demands of the most discriminating buyer and it was aimed at the affluent motorist of the day. The four seat tourer was available at £485 and the two seat tourer at £480, alongside these two models there was a two door Salonette selling at £545 and the full four door saloon for £555. They were expensive motor cars but they were beautifully engineered and luxuriously appointed and were competitively priced when compared to Alvis's, Lagondas and Bentleys of the era. It was becoming apparent that if public interest was to be maintained in the new MG marque that a new model was needed, hence the launch of the 18/80 model. The significance of the 18/80 was that it was the first 'real' MG because the earlier flat radiator and bull nosed cars held such close ties with the Morris equivalents and Cecil Kimber had up until then been charged with upgrading the Morris's to give them wider appeal. The new 18/80 was a car that could be described as a marque on its own as the vast majority of the mechanical components were totally different to those of the current Morris.

It was earlier, during 1927, that the Morris Light Six was announced which was powered by a two and a half litre, six cylinder engine. An unusual departure for Morris was the fact that the camshaft was above the valves operating through 'L' shaped rockers. However the car did not reach the production lines and this particular power unit was eventually used in the Morris Major and after that in the Isis. The chassis of the Morris Light Six was not sufficiently rigid enough to cope with stresses imposed by the powerful 60bhp engine and was redesigned and renamed the Morris Six with little better results. Kimber however saw the potential of this engine for the 18/80 project and Morris Garages purchased a Light Six fabric saloon for evaluation. A brand new chassis frame was made and it was the first time that a chassis unique to MG was produced, all previous ones had been based on the standard Morris chassis. By the time of the 1928 Motor Show, the Light Six engine had been modified with a new block to accommodate twin carburettors that were mounted low down underneath the exhaust manifold with the inlet passing through the block and up to the ports in the head. The cylinder block and crankcase were made in one single casting with a separate cylinder head. A strong 4 main bearing crankshaft was employed with a Duplex chain and

gear drive to the camshaft tensioned by a spring loaded eccentric tensioner. The chain was also utilised to drive the distributor, water pump, oil pump and dynamo all via a single skew gear shaft which occasionally led to running problems. The very latest shell-type big end and main bearings were used which contributed to the very smooth and quiet running of the power unit.

The 18/80 was beautifully constructed with painstaking attention to detail even the bulkhead support brackets incorporated a fine MG motif set into the aluminium. Unfortunately these were hidden from view when the bodywork was mounted onto the chassis. Front and rear axles were designed by MG and utilised Perrot type brake gear. Marles steering sear was used and early prototypes had 14/40 type bolt on wheels, however, all the production cars employed Rudge-Whitworth centre-lock wire spoke wheels. The dashboard displayed quality Jaeger instrumentation whilst the steering wheel was adjustable for rake. Behind the dashboard and mounted on the engine side of the bulkhead was a reserve petrol tank and an oil tank of one gallon capacity which fed oil directly into the crankcase. For the first time a fly-off handbrake was used, mounted inboard on the tourer and saloon versions but externally on the speed twin model. Probably the most noticeable feature however was the distinctive new radiator design with the vertical colour-keyed slats and MG Octagon. This basic design of radiator grille was to be used on MGs throughout the years right up to the end of the T series cars.

Upon introduction the basic price of the chassis only was £420, the buyer could then specify either a tourer or saloon body. The tourer cost a mere £65 extra and the saloon another £135 which by today's standards seems very cheap! The tourer was endowed with a fairly light body compared to the saloon and this allowed pretty brisk acceleration and good top speed compared to the rivals of the day. The MG could easily out accelerate the Lagonda and Alvis models that already held good sporting reputations. In addition to speed the 18/80 had fine responsive steering, excellent road-holding and the three speed gearbox did not prove a drawback due to the good torque characteristics of the engine.

In 1929 a new chassis was designed of much sturdier construction, with a wider track to be designated the Mark II. This was not to replace the Mark I but to sell alongside it and it really must have confused prospective purchasers. The Mark II engaged a track some 4" wider than the Mark I and the already sturdy chassis was considerably strengthened making the new chassis some 330 lbs heavier than its predecessor. The end result was that the Mark II was considerably slower than the Mark I, especially as there was no increase in power from the same engine. This coupled with the fact that the car was priced at £100 more, made the car difficult to sell. Other improvements were the provision of a four speed gearbox, uprated cable operated brakes and bodywork of higher standard incorporating wider mudguards. The chassis, although giving greater rigidity and allowing the use of softer road springs, was a penalty against performance. During 1929 the Mark I was improved, being fitted with uprated cable operated brakes and in 1930 a speed model was introduced. A 'guaranteed' 80mph was claimed for the speed model and a Mark II version was also offered but again suffered with the added weight of the chassis and this detracted from the good acceleration for which the Mark I was admired. Probably the ultimate 18/80 was the Mark III which was an attempt to turn this fine vehicle into a racing car. It was loosely based on the Bentley racing models of the day and constructed on the Mark II, 18/80 chassis. The engine was modified and had a cross flow head, the first time one had been used on an MG. A new crankshaft, camshaft and pistons were fitted and dry sump lubrication completed the package. The model became known as the 18/80 'Tigresse' and variously as the 18/100 because of attempts that were never realised to try and produce 100bhp and 100mph. The car certainly looked the part with its outside exhaust ending in the obligatory fishtail, cycle wings, louvred chassis panels and leather bonnet strap, however weight was again a problem penalising the performance. Competition appearances of the car were few and far between with its first outing in the Brooklands Double Twelve 24 hour race in 1930, ending in disaster. The engine seized after running its bearings and to make matters worse an MG Midget managed to stay the course and finish with a team prize. There was very little public interest shown in the ready-to-race Mark III and only five cars were ever produced, somewhat less than the 25 that Cecil Kimber had hoped for. It was hardly surprising considering the cars carried a £895 price tag. The Mark I stayed in production until early 1931 and the Mark II continued through into 1932. New models were available from stock up until 1934, selling very slowly. This was a reflection of the depressed state of the world economy rather than on the car itself.

# 18/80 Twin door Salonette Mk 1

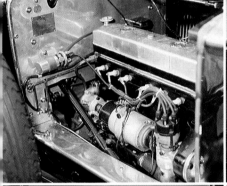

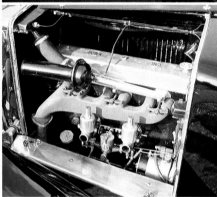

**SPECIFICATION**

Engine

Number of cylinders: 6 in line.

Bore and Stroke: 69mm x 110mm

Capacity: 2468cc

Valve operation: Chain driven, single overhead camshaft.

Carburation: Twin horizontal SUs.

Power output: 60bhp @ 3,200 rpm.

Drive Train

Clutch: Double plate, cork inset, automatically lubricated.

Transmission: Manual crash, 3 forward speeds.

Suspension: Semi elliptic front and rear.

Steering: Marles frictionless gear.

Brakes: 12" drum, Perrot type (early cars) Cable operated (later cars).

Wheels: Centre Lock wire spoke.

Wheelbase: 9' 6"

Track: 4' 0"

Performance: Max speed: approx 80 mph

MPG; approx 18.

Built: MK1: Late 1928 to mid 1931.

Numbers built: 500 of all body variants.

# 18/80 Mk2 Carlton

It has been said that the MG Six or 18/80 as it is better known, was the first real MG and readily identifiable as such. Its forerunners were firmly entrenched in the Morris camp and bore a very close resemblance to their Morris equivalent. It was the 18/80 and the pretty little M type Midget that set the scene with Cecil Kimber giving the cars their own true MG identity. The bull nosed radiators of the 14/28s and the flat radiators of the 14/40s gave way to a new very distinctive chrome plated radiator shell with vertical slats and the MG badge proudly mounted on its own plinth that incorporated the octagonal radiator cap. Kimber had decided that the MGs must be demonstrably different to any of the current Morris models and it was certainly the case with the arrival of the 18/80 in 1928. The new car carried many mechanical components that were totally different to Morris although it was felt by

bearings were used which contributed to the very smooth and quiet running of the unit. The overhead camshaft was driven by a long duplex roller chain with a spring loaded eccentric tensioner and every bearing was oil fed under pressure with an additional feed to the cork clutch. Each valve rocker had its own oil feed as well. To allow for a longer dwell on the ignition, the distributor had a twin contact breaker arrangement whilst on the cosmetic side, many of the engine components such as the dynamo, rocker cover etc. were beautifully finished in polished aluminium. This attention to detail was carried through even to the bulk head support brackets which incorporated a fine MG motif set into the cast aluminium. Some would say that this particular embellishment was wasted in as much as by the time the body was set onto the chassis the motif could not be seen at all!. Two bulkhead tanks

were fitted, one for the reserve petrol tank and the other for the engine oil reservoir.

For the first time on an MG, a racing type fly-off handbrake was fitted mounted externally on the Speed Twin model and inboard on the Tourer and Saloons, whilst the wheels followed the best racing practice and were of Rudge Whitworth centre lock wire spoke design. All pedals and steering were fully adjustable to allow for the most comfortable driving position whilst the dashboard displayed the most comprehensive quality Jaeger instrumentation available, all mounted in a crackle black finished fascia panel. The most distinctive feature of the 18/80 was the aforementioned new radiator shell design which had vertical colour keyed slats that on some cars were able to pivot in unison to either increase or restrict airflow through the radiator dependent on the ambient temperature. Upon introduction the basic price of the 18/80 chassis was £420 and the buyer could specify either a Tourer or Salonette body at £485 and £555 respectively. The two door version of the Tourer was only £5 less and the two door Salonette was £10 cheaper. The Tourer was endowed with a relatively light body compared to the Salonette and as such was able to turn in reasonable performance figures. Contemporary road tests appearing in the motoring magazines were full of praise for the 18/80 and the car fared extremely well up against such rivals as the 3 litre Lagonda,

many that the engine was pure Morris Isis. This was not strictly true for although it was based on the 2.5 litre ohc, six cylinder Morris engine that first appeared in the Morris Light Six, it was quite radically different. For some inexplicable reason, although the Light Six was announced at the 1927 Motor Show, the car never came to production, withdrawn because of shortcomings in the chassis design. The chassis was revamped and the car was renamed the Morris Six, only to be very soon replaced in late 1929 by the very pedestrian Morris Isis.

Kimber purchased a redundant Light Six Fabric Saloon in December 1927 from Morris for evaluation purposes, convinced that something could be made of the engine for his ensuing 14/40 replacement. Due to the problems encountered with the Morris chassis, a brand new chassis was designed and this was to be the first time that a chassis unique to MG had been produced, all previous MGs had utilised standard Morris chassis. By the time of the 1928 Motor Show, the Light Six engine had been extensively modified with a new block to accommodate twin carburettors. These were mounted low down underneath the exhaust manifold with the inlet passing through the block and up to the ports in the head. The cylinder block and crankcase were made in one single casting with a separate cylinder head. The latest shell-type big end and main

which it could out accelerate or the Alvis Silver Eagle, which it was considered had poorer steering and roadholding. Top speed was over 80 mph which was quite exceptional performance in those days considering the size and overall weight of the car. MG 993 is a superbly restored example of an 18/80 and this particular model featured is a very rare 1931 Carlton bodied Mark II drophead coupe with a three-position hood which is owned by Ron Gammons.

# 18/80 MK II CARLTON

Coachwork By THE CARLTON CARRIAGE Co LTD

MG 993

SPECIFICATION

Engine Number of cylinders: 6 in line.

Bore & Stoke: 69 mm x 110 mm.

Capacity: 2468 cc.

Valve operation: Chain driven single overhead camshaft.

Carburation: Twin horizontal SU's. Power output: 60 bhp @ 3,200 rpm.

Clutch: Double plate, cork inset running in oil.

Transmission: Manual "crash" gearbox with 4 forward speeds. Suspension: Semi-elliptic springs front & rear.

Steering: Marles frictionless gear.

Brakes: 12" Drum cable operated.

Wheels: Rudge Whitworth centre-lock wire spoke.

Max speed: Approx 80 mph.

Wheelbase: 9' 6".

Number built (Carlton bodied): Uncertain. Either 4 or 5.

# 18/80 Mk2 Speed Model

The 18/80 MG Six Sports Mark II Speed Model (to give it its' full title) was described by the MG Car Company in their sales brochure as 'a magnificent car which definitely ranks with the most expensive productions today'. I am sure that this statement was very true back in 1932, which was when this marvellous example left the production line at Abingdon. The brochure goes on to describe the car as 'a really fast competition car that may also be driven with comfort and enjoyment as a more-than-ordinary fast touring car. It will cruise indefinitely at sixty and the constant mesh third gear gives a power of acceleration that is a sheer joy to exercise - fifty in a flash!'. Potential customers for this fine vehicle were undoubtedly attracted by the price which was £630 ex-works. The car compared very favourably with contemporary sporting rivals as it offered more refinement and a better top speed than the Lagonda or

Alvis with over 80 mph being attainable. It could also out accelerate them which made the Speed model very attractive, especially as it was some £150 cheaper than its nearest

competitor.

It can be said that the 18/80 was probably the first MG in the style that was to become its hallmark. Earlier bullnosed MGs were very similar to the Morris from which they were derived but from the introduction of the 18/80 Mk I in late 1928, the 'flat nose' radiator which was used as an interim measure on the 14/40, was replaced with the traditional MG slatted grille. This basic design which incorporated the octagon badge in the centre and octagonal radiator cap was to remain right through to the end of the T series production in 1955.

Cecil Kimbers idea was to produce a car which was something in its own right and to get away from the striking similarity of previous models to the Morris derivatives. With the 18/80, most of the mechanical components were new and different to any of the then current Morris models. The engine was a 2468cc unit, with 6 cylinders and an overhead camshaft. This engine did in fact first appear in a Morris chassis known as the Morris Light Six, however the chassis of this car was not up to the stresses imposed by the powerful 60 bhp engine. This car was redesigned and renamed the Morris Six with little better results.

Kimber was convinced that this fine engine could be utilised in an MG, hence the 18/80 was produced and announced at the 1928 Motor Show. The engine received some modification to allow twin carburettors and a stronger camshaft was employed which was driven by a duplex roller chain with spring

tensioner. The latest shell-type big end and main bearings were used, which helped make the engine very smooth running and very quiet. A brand new chassis was designed which for the first time was totally MG, although based on the earlier 14/40 pattern, it was of far sturdier construction. The axles were designed by MG and utilised Perrot type brake gear. Marles steering was used and

early prototypes had 14/40 bolt on wheels, however all the production cars employed Rudge Whitworth centre lock wire wheels. Coachwork, particularly on the speed model featured here, was both luxurious and very well finished. It was beautifully constructed with painstaking attention to detail, even the bulkhead supports, which could not be seen when the bodywork was fitted, incorporated a cut out MG motif set into the aluminium.

The dashboard supported quality Jaeger instrumentation and the steering column was adjustable for rake. Behind the dashboard was mounted a reserve petrol tank and an oil tank with one gallon capacity, feeding oil direct into the crankcase. For the first time a fly-off hand-brake was used and on the car featured, due to the narrow construction of the body, it was mounted on the outside. This particular Mark II Speed Model is believed to be one of only 6 produced in 1932. It differed from the earlier Mark I by employing a four speed as opposed to three speed gearbox and had improved cable operated brakes. The idea was to produce the Mark II version alongside the Mark I version, which really confused the market. The Mark II engaged a wider track, some 4" wider than the Mark I and the chassis already very robust was strengthened even more, thus making it a lot heavier than its predecessor by some 330lbs. The end result was that the Mark II was considerably slower than the Mark I particularly as there was no increase in power from the same engine, coupled with the fact that it sold for £100 more made the car difficult to sell. Probably the ultimate 18/80 was the Mark III, although it was intended as a racing car in the Bentley tradition and was based on the Mark II chassis. The engine was a modified version and had a crossflow head for the first time on a MG. The model became known as the 18/80 "Tigresse" and variously as the 18/100 because of attempts which were never realised to try and produce 100bhp and 100 mph. The interesting thing about the car featured is the fact that although it is a Mark II model, it has a "Tigresse" body which is very rare and it is thought that there are only two surviving examples today.

# 18/80 Mk II SPEED MODEL

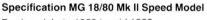

## Specification MG 18/80 Mk II Speed Model

Produced: Late 1929 to mid 1933
Number Built: 6

### Engine:

Number of cylinders: 6 in line
Bore/stroke: 69mm x 110mm
CC: 2468cc
Valve Operation: Chain driven overhead camshaft
Carburation: Twin horizontal SU's
Power output: 60 bhp at 3200 rpm

### Drive Train

Clutch: Double plate, Cork inset, automatically lubricated.
Transmission: Manual ''crash'' with four forward speeds.
Suspension: Half eliptic front and rear
Steering: Marles frictionless gear.
Brakes: 14'' Drum cable operated with servo assistance.
Wheels: Rudge-Whitworth racing type wire wheels 29'' x 5'' with 5'' x 19'' tyres.
Track: 4' 4''
Wheelbase: 9' 6''
Width: 5' 4''
Length: 13' 0''
Weight: 27 cwts.
Price in 1930: £630 ex works

### Performance

Maximum Speed: Approx 80 mph
MPG: Approx 18.

# 18/100 Mk3 Tigresse

Probably the rarest of all MGs and the first to be produced by the MG Car Company specifically for racing is the 18/100 MG Six Mark III Road Racing Model (to give it its full title). Nicknamed the Tigresse, only 5 were ever built by the factory out of a total of 25 that were planned and to this day only 2 are known to have survived. The Mark III was produced to fulfil the demand for a high performance version of the Mark II Sports Six in order to compete in road racing and was inspired by the wonderful 4.5 litre Sports Bentleys of the era. In late 1929, at the time of the move from Oxford to Abingdon, the MG Car Company had two models in production, those being the little M type Midget and the sedate 2.5 litre Mark I. They were both very popular cars but the Mark I was very soon superseded by the Mark II and this car rapidly had a strong following. As a result of Cecil Kimber's desire to see MG represented in competition and a demand from sports-minded enthusiasts, the first MG built specifically for competition was born in the form of the 18/100 Mark III.

The Abingdon engineers set about the task of transforming the Mark II into the Mark III with much enthusiasm. This entailed major work, particularly with the engine and although the same block and cubic capacity of 2468 cc were retained for manufacturing reasons, this is where the similarity ended. A comprehensive re-work of the engine was undertaken which involved an extensively modified four bearing crankshaft and machined connecting rods in conjunction with special waisted pistons. All components were individually balanced statically and dynamically and polished to facilitate flaw detection. A new twin spark plug cylinder head was produced of crossflow design with internally machined ports and specially shaped combustion chambers that gave a compression ratio of 6.9:1. Two separate induction passages fed two groups of three cylinders each with two sparking plugs per cylinder. Fuel/air mixture was fed to the two inlet ports from a pair of specially designed SU downdraught carburettors that had unique egg-shaped dashpots. Oil breather pipes were directed from the top cover to the mouths of the carburettors to permit oil vapour to be drawn in through the carburettors to give upper cylinder lubrication. A new type overhead camshaft chain driven from the crankshaft gave considerably more valve overlap than on the Mark II engine.

The engine lubrication was by means of a dry sump system with a large capacity 5 gallon tank situated between the front dumb irons in order to aid cooling. A twin oil pump circulated the oil under 80 lbs pressure to the engine bearings by means of internal galleries. The tank had a central tube installed through which the starting handle could be passed. On the cooling side a new centrifugal pump circulated 5 gallons of coolant round the engine and radiator. The last of the fluids to be accommodated was the petrol which was contained in a special 28 gallon tank situated beneath the rear seat just ahead of the rear axle and was sited as low in the chassis as possible to aid weight distribution. Huge fillers adorned each side of the tank which enabled

rapid replenishment under competition conditions and the fuel was fed to the carburettors via two Autopulse electric pumps. Ignition was again unique to the Mark III and by means of a huge Lucas twin spark distributor. Each cylinder had two spark plugs that fired simultaneously via twin coils mounted each side of the dynamo.

With the emphasis on racing and the need for rapid gear changes a new type of clutch was employed of single plate cork insert design

running in oil. Power was transferred through a close ratio four speed gearbox with a choice of final drive ratios available. Also in keeping with the high level of preparation for competition, all steering gear and brake components were draw filed and polished to aid flaw detection. Special attention was given to the brakes whereby drums of 14" diameter were employed giving a total effective braking area of 208 sq inches, whilst the drums were heavily ribbed to aid cooling. The fly-off hand brake was mounted externally as was an ingenious handwheel for adjustment of the brakes whilst

the car was in motion on long distance road races.

The chassis consisted of deep channel side members swept up at the front and rear and joined in the centre by two channel section cross members that in turn were united by a large diameter tubular member through which the propeller shaft passed. Semi elliptic leaf springs were shackled at the front and pinned at their rear whilst the rear springs were mounted in Silentbloc bushes. The front springs were automatically lubricated at high pressure from the central lubrication system. There were two large double Hartford friction dampers fitted to the front whilst at the rear, there were no less than four dampers fitted with one pair being set at right angles to the other.

To quote the MG Car Company's own sales literature: "No expense has been spared to produce the finest road racing machine of its class. Such are the manufacturing facilities at our disposal, that it is possible to offer a car fully prepared and equipped for the most arduous event at a figure never before approached. Everything that the most exacting racing motorist requires is embodied in the MG Six Sports Mark III. You can buy it ready for racing with no further preparation. Bearings are free, brakes bedded in, vital axle and steering parts draw filed to make sure no hidden flaws exist, nuts split pinned or wired and to borrow a sporting simile, "trained to the last hair". It is complete with a well made four seater body, conforming to existing International Road Racing Regulations, this being the only style of coachwork with which it is supplied. The keynote of the MG Sports Six Mark III is utter controllability at the highest speeds, a degree of roadworthiness never before approached and with powers of acceleration and speed that do not belie its name, yet tractable enough to make the most delightful fast tourer for which the sportsman could wish".

The car certainly looked the part with its external exhaust ending in the obligatory Brooklands fishtail, cycle wings, louvred body panels and leather bonnet strap, but weight penalised performance and actual competition appearances were few and far between. The first outing at the Brooklands Double Twelve 24 hour race in 1930 ended in disaster with the engine failing after a carburettor butterfly came loose and was drawn into the head. To make matters worse an M type Midget stayed the course and finished with a team prize. Unfortunately there was little public interest in the car and only five were ever produced, which is of little surprise considering its price tag of £895. This really was a reflection of the depressed state of the world economy at the time rather than condemnation of the car itself. It is believed, although not confirmed, that the car featured, JB 855 was originally owned by Cecil Kimber. It is now owned, along with the only other known to survive, GH 3501, by Chris Barker of Winchester.

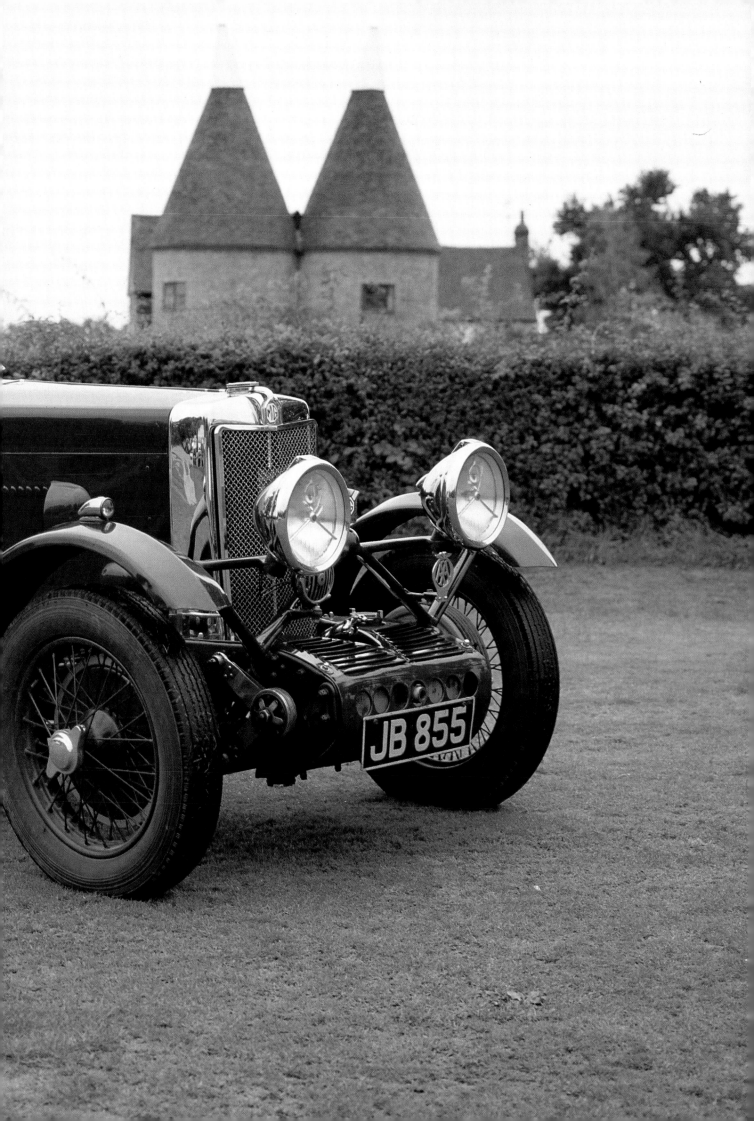

# 18/100 Mk III TIGRESS

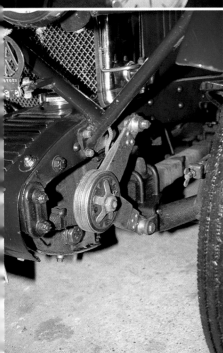

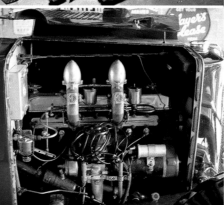

## SPECIFICATION

**Engine**
Number of cylinders: 6 in line.
**Bore & Stroke:** 69mm x 110mm.
**Capacity:** 2468 cc.
**Valve operation:** Chain driven single overhead camshaft.
**Carburation:** Special twin SU carburettors.
**Transmission:** Four speed non-synchromesh with remote control.
**Clutch:** Single plate cork insert running in oil.
**Chassis:** Steel channel with rivetted cross-members.
**Suspension:** Semi-elliptic front & rear. Double Hartford friction shock absorbers. Two at front, four at rear.
**Brakes:** Cable & rod operated with 14" drums.
**Wheels:** Centre lock wire spoke with racing rims. 19" dia.
**Wheelbase:** 9' 6".
**Track:** 4' 4".
**Weight:** 26.25 cwts.
**Body:** Open four seater
**Number built:** 5.
Price new in 1930: £895.

# M Type Midget
# Abingdon Works Van Replica

An unusual subject is a faithful reproduction of the M type Midget based delivery van that Cecil Kimber had built as a promotional vehicle in the 1930s. Resplendent in its brown and cream livery and distinctive signwriting, the original vehicle would have been prominent at all the major race circuits and competition venues where MGs were competing. The 'High Speed' Service Van as it was known was the source of some ridicule by racegoers and the like by pure fact that in the thirties there were speed restrictions that limited commercial vehicles to 30mph, however Kimber could have argued that the signwriting referred to the vehicles that the van was there to service!

There is no doubt that the M type Midget was the first of a long line of MGs that was to make the MG so popular throughout the world and although the Kimber promotional van was short lived the M type was to prove very popular with over 3,235 models being produced between 1929 and 1932. The M type was loosely based on the Morris Minor and Kimber seized the opportunity to produce this sporty model to compete with the Austin Seven which had been introduced some years earlier in 1923 and was performing well in racing

events. As with previous MGs the M type utilised many Morris components with one or two minor modifications and although launched with great success at the 1928 Motor Show at Olympia, the car did not go into full production until 1929. The main differences over the Morris extended to the narrowing of

the body and the exterior fittings. The reason for the similarity between the Minor and the Midget was the fact that Kimber desperately wanted to get the car on display at Olympia and there was not sufficient time to get exclusive MG components designed and made. Nonetheless there were tremendous initial demands for the car and it sold well for the ensuing three years.

The standard M type body was designed and fabricated by Carbodies of Coventry and was a fairly simple affair being very light and of fabric construction on a wooden frame with the distinctive boat tailed rear. These bodies were made at Coventry then shipped to Abingdon for fitting to the chassis. The engine was a four cylinder unit with a two bearing crankshaft and had an overhead camshaft driven through two sets of bevel gears and a vertical shaft. This shaft passed through the vertically mounted dynamo and doubled as the armature with a flexible coupling transferring the drive from the armature to the cylinder head via a short shaft. The sturdy little 20 horsepower engine proved to be very reliable and the same basic design of engine was incorporated in the subsequent Magna and Magnette range of the era and contributed to the success of these cars. The axles, chassis and clutch were all 'borrowed' from Morris, although the steering was modified with the column being more steeply raked and the springs had decreased camber. The remote control gear change was angled downward to give a better and lower driving position than on the Morris. The whole car then took on a more sporty appearance than its rivals and this coupled with the fact that it had good roadholding and better performance together with a price tag of 185 meant that it sold very well indeed.

Much of the enthusiasm for this little car was

generated from the tremendous upsurge in interest for Motor Sport and the increase in participation by owners of such cars as the M type. The car weighed in at a mere 10 cwts and with 20 horsepower available from the willing engine the cars simply flew with 60mph being achieved very quickly. Motoring magazines of the era were full of praise for this little MG and sports car history was in the making. Autocar are quoted as saying, "Sixty or sixty five miles an hour are not adventure but delight, acceleration is very brisk, altogether an extraordinary fascinating vehicle." Kimber felt that due to the success of private individuals in racing, the time was right to channel some effort into competition and he was soon to realise the full benefits and the sales potential of winning competitions with cars bearing the famous MG octagon. The decision was taken to form a competitions department at Abingdon and their brief was to develop the M type. In 1930 an additional 7 horsepower was extracted from the 847cc engine and a works team was entered for the Brooklands Double Twelve Race. These cars had special Brooklands exhaust systems, larger fuel tanks and slightly revised bodies with lower cutaway doors. Although some of their rivals had a distinct power advantage the MGs endured long hours at high speed to be rewarded with the Team prize.

Proudly displayed on the rear doors of the High Speed van the slogan 'Safety Fast!' was adopted by Kimber in 1930 to generate a theme that still exists to this day. It was this clever and precise promotional slogan that inspired many intending customers to purchase the MG products of the day, particularly the M type Midget. During its production span many improvements were made and after appearing at the 1931 Motor Show for the fourth time, the car was eventually phased out in 1932. During production several special cars were produced for record breaking purposes and in 1930 a car codenamed EX 120 was made ready for the attack on the Class H speed record. Captain George Eyston was to successfully drive the car at the Montlhery track in France at over 100mph in February 1931, much to the delight of Kimber and the Abingdon workforce. Following in the success of Eyston's run, a special Midget was produced for the racing orientated owner, this was designated the C type Midget but was to become better known as the Montlhery Midget

High MG Speed
Service Van

M.G. Car Company Ltd.
...avlova Works,
...on on Thames.

# M Type
## Replica Works Van

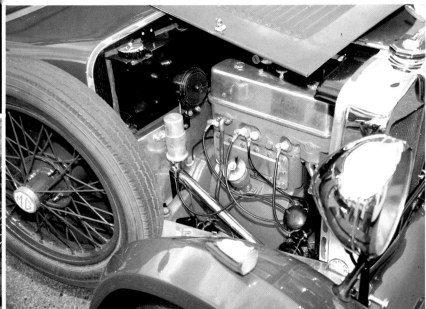

SPECIFICATION
Engine
Type: In line water cooled.
No of cylinders: 4
Bore/stroke: 57mm × 73mm.
Capacity: 746cc.
Valve operation: Overhead camshaft driven through vertical dynamo.
Carburation: Single SU automatic piston type.
Power output: Dependent on state of tune; between 37.4bhp and 52.5bhp.
Drive Train
Clutch: Single dry plate.
Transmission: Manual crash 3 forward speeds and reverse.
Chassis
Frame: Twin side members, tapered and upswept front & rear.
Wheelbase: 6' 6"
Track 3' 6" front and rear.
Suspension: semi elliptic shackled front and rear with Hartford friction dampers.
Brakes: 8" drum cable operated.
Tyres: 27" × 4"
Wheels: Wire spoke bolt on.
Number produced: 1, but total of M types 1929-1931; 3235

# M Type Midget Double Twelve Replica

It is surprising to think that the Sports Austin Seven may have been partly responsible for the concept of the highly popular and successful M Type Midget, the car that many people think made the Abingdon-located Company truly established in the field of sports-car competitions. Until 1928, most of the MGs that had been produced were basically touring cars, with the accent on comfort and average speeds rather than torque and high performance. Cecil Kimber saw however, that the Sports Austin Seven presented a real rival in the car market, and immediately set forth to design a competitor, recognising the fact that his customers were looking for a fun 'racey' looking vehicle, rather than a high-priced sports car.

The M Type Midget emerged in time to make its debut at the 1928 Olympia Motor Show, based in concept on the Morris Minor. The recently designed two-seater body was just put upon the Minor chassis, as well as using the clutch and axle system, which a lot of people thought was done in order for the car to meet the tight deadline of '28 Olympia, as numerous improving modifications soon followed. The engine in the original M Type was four cylinder, with a two bearing crankshaft. The overhead camshaft was powered by two sets of bevel gears and a vertical shaft, this shaft being made up partly by the dynamo armature. To convey the drive from the armature to the cylinder head, a flexible coupling was used, whilst the bearings were of white metal with the exception of the front crank bearing, which was a double-row ball race. To give extra support, the main bearings were supported by the crankcase, as the crankshaft went into the case by the front-end.

With regard to the porting on the M Type, this was found along the left hand side of the cylinder head, the inlets joining together, and this also applied to cylinders 2 and 3 exhaust opening. The valves were moved by long thin cam followers, and leaned inwards slightly, turning round on bushes on shafts, found each side of the head. This was a design feature that proved to be successful on all the overhead camshaft Midgets, Magnas and Magnettes.

Kimber indeed read the market well, as this original M Type proved to be relatively cheap to buy, economical to run, extremely reliable, and became a proven successful competitor in many aspects of motor sport. Although it did not set out to be a sports car in type originally, the M Type was soon established, through its excellent roadholding and speed, as a 'true sports car' by the media soon after its release. The successes of the M Type were found in the 1930 Monte Carlo Rally, where it finished well up in its class, a record holder for the 1100cc class in the Mont des Mules hillclimb, as well as a total of 18 winning Gold Medals in the Land's End Trial. Of course, many other achievements have been recorded, but the M Type is most notable for its success in the Brookland's Double Twelve Race in 1930, of which the featured car is one of only 30 replicas made from the winning specification.

The Double Twelve was a twenty four hour race, held on the steeply banked curves of Brooklands, and was a highly prestigious race to win. Ranked with Le Mans, competition was fierce, and endurance and reliability was the name of the game to win this one. For the 1930 race, Kimber had produced a huge 'tiger' of a car, the big 18/100 Mark III, but was asked by two friends if they may also enter three Midgets in the race for the team prize, just as work on the Mk III was nearly finished. Kimber agreed, and allocated Reg Jackson to help with the M Type Midget; Jackson already knew well the peculiarities of the car, as he had been working on the 'teething' troubles during the vehicle's first year of production. The braking system had always been a 'weak link' in the structure of the otherwise popular and good selling Midget, and Jackson had finally cured the car of this misdemeanour; now his orders were to make the little car go faster!

Most of Kimber's energies were still pouring into the Mark III, but N. H. Charles, MGs expert on design and development, began to take an interest in the M Type. Jackson had been polishing the engine with a metal polish called 'Shinio', hoping to stave off metal fatigue and fragmentation during this 24-hour race, and inevitably, the name Shinio was soon given as a nickname to the M Type. With Charles's expertise, the minute Shinio got an instant power increase to from 20bhp to 27bhp. This was achieved by increasing the usual rev. range of the engine, with improved valve timing and larger carburettors. A regulation Brookland's exhaust system was fitted, and a slightly bigger fuel tank was added to give greater distance during the 24 hours. Five cars in total were prepared, and apart from the mentioned engine modifications, were entered almost as standard. A purist would notice that the bodywork was slightly narrower, the door sides were cut away more deeply, bonnet-straps (compulsory for racing at Brooklands) were added, stronger wheels fitted and also a folding gauze windscreen as preparation for the Double Twelve, but otherwise the car was as it would be sold for use on the open road.

Two of the race prepared M Types were for privateers, but the remaining three were for the 'friends' of Kimber who first approached him about this Midget Team - Edmondson and Randall. MG quickly dubbed the team 'The Tomato Growers' as the two drivers had their business interests in market gardening! Another Midget had also entered the 1930 Double Twelve, but as a private entry. Soon after the start of the race, the much thought of Mark II 'blew up'. This was obviously a great disappointment to Kimber, and long diagnoses were held. The drivers, Callingham and Parker, considered that a throttle butterfly had come loose and clearly described the moment

to a motoring journalist: "When we took the sump off the crankshaft was purple. There wasn't a bearing left anywhere."

Compensation, however, must have been found with the faithful little M Type Midgets. With the exception of the private entry that retired at the end of the first day, all ran fluently and perfectly. At the end of the second day, an average speed of 60.23 mph had been achieved by the Midget driven by Randall Montgomery (who also drove the car at Monte Carlo), and was good enough to take a notable fourteenth place overall. The other four also reached the finish, giving the 'Tomato Growers' the team prize, ahead of their main rivals - The Works Austin Sevens! This was considered a truly great achievement for such a small car, and certainly put the Abingdon Works 'on the map' for competition sports cars. To commemorate this performance, thirty replicas of the 'Double Twelve M Types' were produced. Finished in the original colours of cream and brown, this car is one of only a few left from the 30 replicas made.

After the achievement at Brooklands, the Midget again appeared at the 1930 Olympia Motor Show, this time with the Double Twelve valve timing, and other improvements. The car stayed in production until 1932, with 3,253 being built in total. Although superceeded in time, the original M Type and its Double Twelve modifications influenced many of its successors in design for many years to follow.

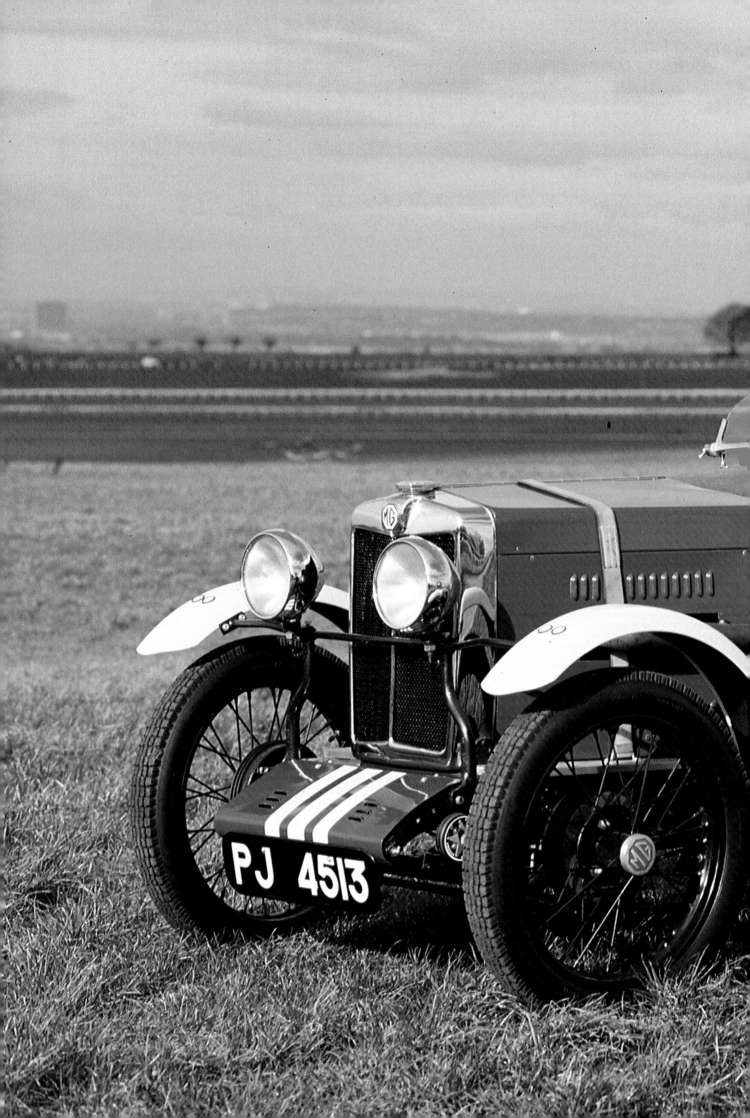

# M TYPE
## DOUBLE TWELVE
### Replica

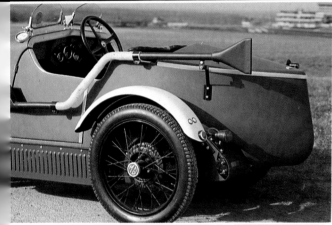

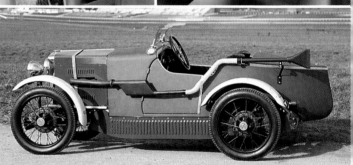

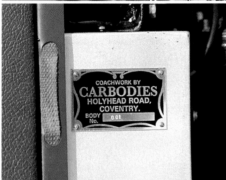

COACHWORK BY
**CARBODIES**
HOLYHEAD ROAD,
COVENTRY.
BODY No. 001

**Specification**
Engine
Number of cylinder: 4
Capacity: 847cc
Valve operation: Single overhead cam
Approx power: 20bhp early cars 27bhp Double Twelve and late cars.
Brakes: 8″ diameter mechanically operated cable brakes
Max Speed: 60.23mph
Numbers produced: 3,253 built, 30 'Double Twelve' replicas produced between late 1928-1932.
Models: Double Twelve Replicas
Open top two-seater
Saloon two-seater
Price: £245.00

# M Type Midget

The MG M Type Midget was undoubtably the first of a long line of MGs that were to make the sports car so popular throughout the world and it is almost impossible to overestimate the importance of the little car in this respect. The introduction of the Morris Minor in 1928 by William Morris obviously got Cecil Kimber thinking especially as another rival Herbert Austin had his Austin Seven well established in the market place. The Seven was introduced in 1923 and was doing well in racing events. The Morris Minor appeared five years after and was seen to be a worthy competitor

with an overhead camshaft engine based on a design originally introduced on Wolseleys, whereas the Austin simply had a sidevalve engine.

Cecil Kimber soon grasped the idea of producing an MG sports car based on the Morris Minor, since a lot of forerunners were Morris derivatives, this was hardly a surprising move. The M Type Midget was launched at the Motor Show at Olympia in October 1928, it was evident that the car would be a success with the tremendous initial demands at the Show and indeed it sold well for the ensuing three years. The car did not go into full production until 1929 utilising mainly Morris components with slight modifications. The narrow two seater body and its exterior fittings were the main differences. The reason for the similarity was the pressure to get the car on show at Olympia and there was not sufficient time to allow more individual components to be designed and manufactured. The body was a very simple affair being very light and of fabric construction on a wooden frame. The distinctive boat tail design was fabricated separately by Carbodies of Coventry and mated with the chassis at the MG factory in Abingdon.

The engine was a four cylinder unit with a two bearing crankshaft and had an overhead camshaft driven through two sets of bevel gears and a vertical shaft. This shaft passed through the vertically mounted dynamo and doubled as the armature, with a flexible coupling transferring the drive from the armature to the cylinder head via a short shaft. The sturdy little 20 horsepower engine proved to be very reliable and the same basic design of engine was incorporated in the subsequent Magna and Magnette range of the era and was contributory to the success of these cars.

The axles, chassis and clutch were all 'borrowed' from Morris although the springs had decreased camber and the steering was modified with the steering column being more steeply raked. The remote gear change was angled downwards to give a lower driving position than on the Morris. The whole car then took on a more sporty appearance over its competitors coupled with the fact that it had good roadholding and better performance and it retailed at only £185. The car not surprisingly sold like hot cakes! Much of the enthusiasm for the car was due to the sudden growth of

Motor Sport and increased participation from owners of such cars as the M type weighing just 10 cwt and with 20 bhp available the car simply flew with 60 mph being achieved very quickly. Motoring magazines of the time were full of praise for this MG and sports car history was in the making. Autocar are quoted as saying, 'Sixty or Sixty Five miles an hour are not adventure but delight, acceleration is very brisk, altogether an extraordinary fascinating little vehicle'.

Because racing was now indulged in by private individuals successfully this inspired Cecil Kimber to channel efforts into competition for he was soon to realise the full benefits and sales potential of winning competitions with cars bearing the MG badge. A small racing department was formed at Abingdon and their attention and was focused on developing the M type Midget. In 1930 an extra 7 bhp was extracted from the 847 cc engine and a works team of 5 cars was entered for the Brooklands Double Twelve Race. These cars had special Brooklands exhaust systems, larger fuel tanks and slightly revised bodies with lower cutaway doors. Although some of their rivals had a distinct power advantage, the five Midgets endured the long hours at high speed admirably, to be rewarded with the Team Prize at the end.

As a direct result of this prestigious win, a replica Double Twelve M Type was produced and added to the Midget range at £245 which now

also included the Midget Sportsman's Coupe. This particular variant made a great impact upon its introduction and a notable customer was Henry Fords son, Edsel who imported one into the USA which created much interest amongst his fashionable acquaintances.

It was in late 1930 that Cecil Kimber was to adopt the slogan of 'Safety Fast' and this alone inspired intending customers to purchase. Many improvements were made during the production span of the car and after appearing at the 1931 Motor Show for the fourth time, the M Type was eventually phased out in 1932. Over 3235 models had been produced, sadly it is anticipated that only about 150 to 200 survive to this day. Several special Midgets were produced based on the M type for record breaking attempts. During 1930 the factory produced a prototype designated EX 120. this chassis had a 6'9" wheelbase as opposed to 6'6" on the standard card with the main chassis members swept up over the front axle but passed below the rear axle. This project was destined for the Company's first attempt at international speed records.

Well known record breakers of the era, Captain George Eyston and Earnest Eldridge were keen to secure the Class H speed record (for up to 750cc). The M type derived engine was modified from 847 cc to 750 cc, the chassis was fitted with a special pointed tail body and with various other modifications was ready for a record attempt by late 1930. The first attempt failed at the Montlhery track in France, but rapid modifications which included the fitting of a supercharger ensured success. Eyston took the car to over 100 mph on several occasions in February 1931, much to the delight of Cecil Kimber and the Abingdon workforce. Following this success a special Montlhéry Midget was produced for the racing orientated owner, this was designated the C Type, but became better known as the Montlhéry Midget.

# M TYPE

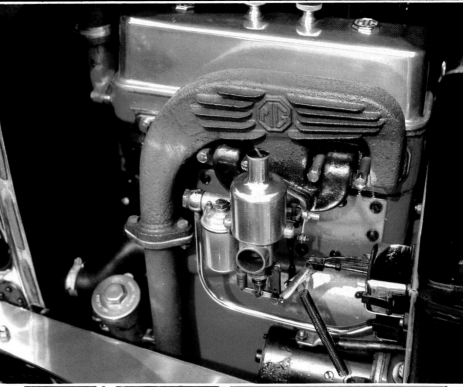

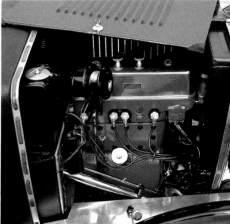

## Specification

### Engine:
Type: In line water cooled.
No of cylinders: 4
Bore/stroke: 57mm x 83mm
Capacity: 847cc
Valve operation: Overhead camshaft driven through vertical dynamo.
Carburation: Single SU automatic piston type with hand mixture control on dash.
Power output: Early cars bhp @ 4000 rpm. Later cars; 27 bhp @ 4500 rpm.

### Drive Train
Clutch: Single dry plate.
Transmission: Manual crash, three forward speeds and reverse.

Chassis
Frame: twin side members, tapered and upswept front and rear with strengthened cross members.
Wheelbase: 6'6"
Track: 3'6" front and rear.
Length: 9'2"
Width: 4'2"
Suspension: semi elliptic shackled front and rear with Hartford friction dampers.
Brakes: 8" drum, cable operated.
Tyre size: 27" x 4"
Wheels: wire spoke

### Performance
Maximum speed: 68 mph
Fuel consumption: 38 mpg approx.
Number Built: 3235
Cost new in 1930: £185. Treasury rating (tax) £8 per annum.

# M Type Midget Jarvis Bodied

There was excitement at the 1928 London Motor Show when MG launched two brand new models. The well established and very popular 14/40 was to be superseded by the MG Sports Six 18/80 which boasted a six cylinder 2468 cc overhead camshaft engine. The 18/80 was to be the first MG to be built on a chassis that did not owe its parentage to Morris as it was designed by Cecil Kimber himself. Other components were modified Morris but essentially this was more of an MG in its own right. The other new model, the M Type Midget, was totally at the other end of the spectrum and quite tiny compared to the 18/80. This new offering from the mews garage that the MG Car Company occupied in Edmund Road, Oxford, was the first of a long line of MGs that were to make the marque so popular throughout the world. It was the Austin Seven that really prompted Kimber to produce the compact M Type for he realised that his customers were quite desperate for an affordable sports car that could rival the Sports Austin Seven. Up until 1928, most MGs had been basically touring cars with the accent on comfort and average speeds rather than high performance coupled with good torque. Kimber therefore designed a competitor for the Austin Seven in the form of the M Type which was deemed a "fun and racy" looking vehicle, rather than a sedate high priced sports tourer. There was great interest in the two MGs, par-

on the Morris Minor, the new Midget differed visually but as with previous MGs the M type utilised many Morris components that were modified to varying degrees. The car was launched with great success and many orders were taken at the show, much to the delight of Kimber. Priced very modestly at £185 the car initially sold very well and also for the ensuing three years with demand outstripping production at times. The success of the Midget along with buoyant sales of other models forced a move to larger premises in the Autumn of 1929 when the MG Car Company moved from their crowded mews garage in the centre of Oxford to the factory formerly occupied by the Pavlova Leather Company at Abingdon-on-Thames.

Kimber was so desperate to get the M type to the Olympia Show that there was not sufficient time to get exclusive MG components made, therefore to make the car look sufficiently different from its stablemate a special body was designed and fabricated by Carbodies of Coventry. It was of fairly simple wooden frame construction and fabric covered which made it very lightweight. The bodies were shipped to Oxford from Coventry and were mated to the standard Minor chassis. Other components "borrowed" from the Morris camp included axles although the springs were modified with decreased camber and Hartford shock absorbers were fitted. The steering gear was altered with the column being more steeply

petition. The motoring press soon established the little car as "a true sports car" and were full of praise for it. Autocar were quoted as saying "Sixty or sixty five miles per hour are not an adventure but a delight, acceleration is very brisk, altogether an extraordinary fascinating vehicle"

Although the Abingdon factory offered a choice of the open two seater or the tiny closed 2 seater fabric bodied Sportman's Coupe and later on a replica of the 'Double Twelve' Midget, a few chassis were acquired by specialist coachbuilders. One such company was the firm of Jarvis and Son of Wimbledon who had been established since 1867 making their name in the construction of fine horse carriages. In the late 1920's the company turned their skills toward the fabrication of special bodies for road and racing cars to their own design. Sir Malcolm Campbell and Wolf Barnato of Bentley fame were just two of the notable customers requiring specialist coachbuilding for their record breaking and racing exploits. It was not until the 1930's that the association with MG was formed. One of the directors of Jarvis, Jimmy Palmes was originally a fellow university student with George Eyston at Cambridge and it was no surprise when Eyston took a seat on the board of directors at Jarvis for what was to be a long and beneficial association. Eyston had successfully broken the 100 mph barrier in EX 120 which was a car specially produced by Abingdon for an attempt on the class H speed record. Shortly after this, Jarvis were to become involved with the design and construction of the successor to EX 120, EX 127 better known as the 'Magic Midget'. Jarvis had carried a Morris franchise since 1925 for the supply of new vehicles and with the work on the record breaking cars came the much desired agency for MG. This latterly extended to Wolseley and Riley as well. The M type Midget was to be their first coachbuilt MG and was without doubt a deluxe version of the car of superior quality that carried the full endorsement of the MG Car Company. The car sold for £225 which was considerably more than the standard boat-tailed Midget which was a modest £185. Nonetheless there was a healthy demand for this type of 'up-market' car and very soon Jarvis were joined in the MG marketplace with offerings from other notable coachbuilders such as Styles, Abbey, Carlton and Vanden Plas to name but a few.

The delightful M type featured is a 1931 Jarvis bodied version owned by Philip Bayne-Powell. This car is particularly rare in as much as it is the only known example with a metal panelled body, also rare is the fabric bodied type of which Philip knows of only one surviving.

ticularly as for the first time they had a new identity in the form of the distinctive MG radiator surround. Gone were the designs simply extended from the Morris range of cars, MG now had its own hallmark which was to stay with the cars in various forms throughout the years. The TF Midget was really the last MG to incorporate the traditional design, although the pattern stayed on, albeit in truncated form, on the MGA, MGB and various saloons in the sixties and seventies. It was the M type Midget however that aroused the greatest interest amongst the visitors to the Motor Show at Olympia, with its boat tailed body, raked V split screen and cycle wings the car certainly looked the part and although the Austin Seven had been around since 1923 and was well established in the market place, this new MG was out to capture a slice of the market that hitherto had been dominated by Austin. Based

raked and the remote gear change was angled downwards to accommodate a lower "more sporty" driving position. The engine was the trusty four cylinder 847 cc unit of Wolseley parentage. It had a two bearing crankshaft and an overhead camshaft driven through two sets of bevel gears and a vertical shaft that formed the armature of the vertically mounted dynamo. With 20 horsepower available from the very willing engine and the car only weighing a mere 10 hundredweight the little MG was quite a performer with 60 mph easily achievable. Kimber had certainly identified the demand accurately and much of the enthusiasm for this little car was generated from the tremendous upsurge in interest for motor sport and the increase in participation by owners of such cars as the M type Midget. The car proved to be totally reliable, economical to run and best of all a very competitive car in com-

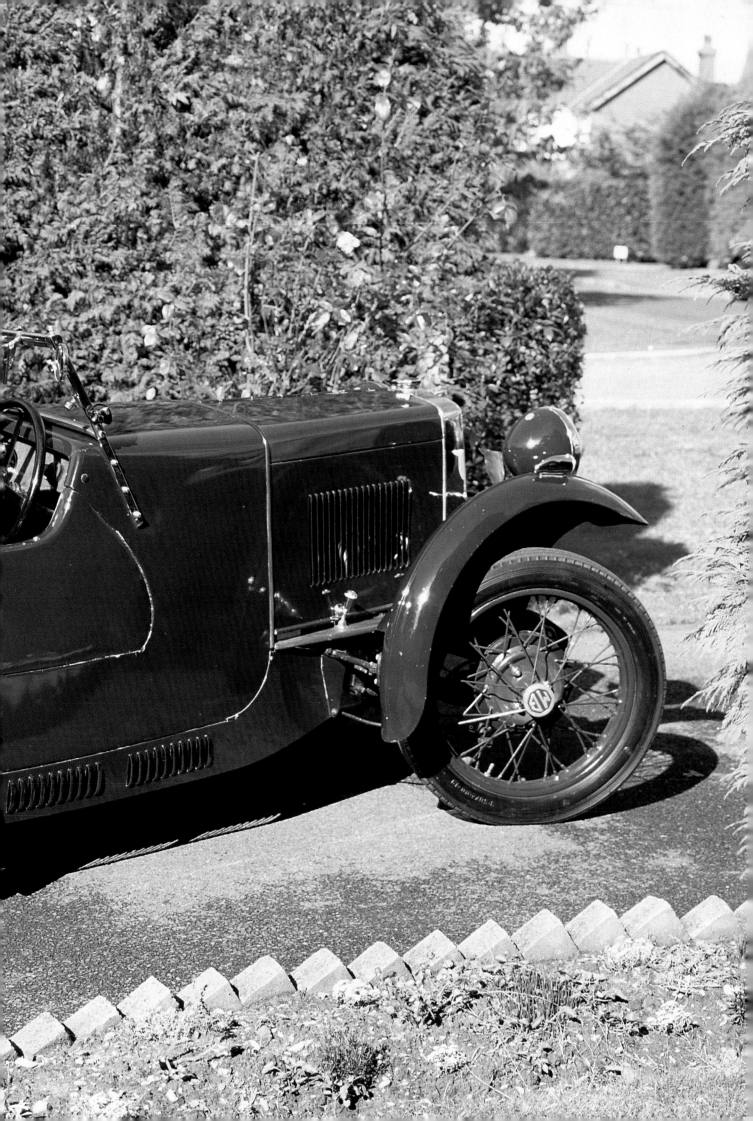

# JARVIS BODIED M TYPE

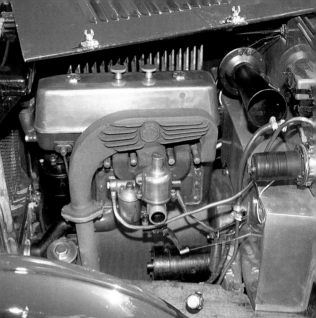

SPECIFICATION
Engine
Type: In line water cooled.
No of cylinders: 4.
Bore & Stroke: 57mm x 83mm.
Capacity: 847cc.
Valve operation: Overhead camshaft driven through vertical dynamo.
Carburation: Single SU automatic piston type.
Power output: Early cars; 20 bhp at 4000 rpm
Later cars; 27 bhp at 4500 rpm
Clutch: Single dry plate.
Transmission: Manual crash, 3 forward speeds and reverse.
Chassis: twin side members, tapered and upswept front and rear with strengthened cross members.
Wheelbase: 6' 6". Track: 3' 6" front and rear.
Suspension: Semi-elliptic shackled front and rear.
Dampers: Hartford friction type.
Brakes: 8" drum cable operated.
Tyres: 27" x 4".
Wheels: Bolt-on wire spoke.
Max speed: 68 mph.
Number built: (all types) 3235.

# C Type Montlhéry Midget

Shortly after its debut at the 1928 Motor Show at Olympia, a sporting version of the little 847 cc 'M' type Midget was produced specifically to compete in the Brooklands Double Twelve endurance race. It was because racing was indulged in by private individuals quite successfully, using fairly standard production cars, that Cecil Kimber decided to channel efforts into a small competitions department at Abingdon. He was very mindful of the tremendous sales potential of offering tuning services to prospective customers and existing ones not to mention the enormous benefits derived from factory backed and privately entered cars winning competitions bearing the MG badge. Earlier attempts by MG to compete with the rather sedate 18/100 in the Double Twelve had proved rather disastrous, but by complete contrast the 'M' type Midget's venture was very successful with the 5 cars storming away with the team prize after an arduous race at high speeds. As a result of this, a Double Twelve replica was made available to the public and with a limited run of 30 cars they were very soon in the hands of enthusiastic amateur racing drivers.

After appearing at the 1931 Motor Show for the fourth time, the 'M' type was eventually phased out in 1932 with over 3,235 models being produced. Several special Midgets were produced specifically for record breaking purposes and during 1930 the Abingdon factory prepared a prototype designated EX 120 and it was this project that was destined for the Company's first attempt at International speed records in the hands of Captain George Eyston and Ernest Eldridge. They were keen to secure the class H speed record for cars up to 750 cc and the capacity of the 'M' type was reduced from 847 cc to 743 cc for this attempt. With a modified chassis and special boat tailed body the car was ready for a record attempt over in France at the Montlhéry track in November 1930. The first attempt failed, but rapid modifications which included the fitting of a supercharger ensured success with Eyston taking the car to over 100 mph on several occasions in February 1931. There was great delight back in Abingdon with the achievement and

following this success Kimber immediately released details of another project for a special racing Midget. Originally designated the 'C' type Midget, it soon became better known as the Montlhéry Midget.

With EX 120 being used as the test bed for future models, the chassis and engine details had been sufficiently proven on the open road and extensively at Brooklands race track for the tooling to be put in hand for the 'C' type and its sports car equivalent the 'D' type. The overriding difference between EX 120 and the new 'C' type was in the bore and stroke of the engine which was to be 57mm x 73mm giving a cubic capacity of 746 cc whilst the new 'D' type retained the same 57mm x 83mm of the 'M' type. A single downdraught carburettor was inherited from the 'M' type and a new innovation on the 'C' type was the installation of a scuttle mounted bulk oil reservoir which was float chamber controlled. Strictly with advantages for competition use it obviated the need for checking the oil at hectic pit stops which generally entailed removing bonnets, checking dipstick levels etc. A set amount of oil could replenish the reservoir very quickly via the scuttle top mounted quick filler and most importantly the correct level of oil was always maintained in the engine sump. This system was of great benefit to the later supercharged cars which were particularly heavy on oil consumption.

The transmission and clutch were chosen mindful of the increased power outputs generated by the more powerful engine and with margins to cope with supercharging on the later cars. A specially developed twin plate clutch transferred power from engine to gearbox which was the hefty ENV 4 speed crash change variety and final drive to the rear wheels was through straight cut spiral bevel gears. The chassis frame was made from straight and parallel steel channel which underslung the rear axle and swept over the front axle. Cross brace tubes passed through the side members and were affixed with brazed flanges, the end result being a very strong yet flexible structure. Semi-elliptic springs were fitted all round that floated at one

end in bronze trunnions. The braking arrangements were cable operated which allowed a system that was unaffected by axle movement and also was not prone to most forms of accidental damage. A racing-type fly-off handbrake was coupled into the same operating system as the footbrake and thus enjoyed the same efficiency. There was independent adjustment of all four brake cam levers via wing nuts and a main handwheel control adjacent to the gear box remote control that allowed adjustment of the brakes whilst the car was in motion. There was also an adjuster by the steering column for the rear André Hartford shock absorbers so they could be trimmed from within the cockpit to compensate for weight reduction as fuel was being used.

The standard body was a two seater aluminium panelled item which had a pointed boat tail similar to the 'M' type. The hinged top panel concealed the spare wheel and the 15 gallon fuel tank which had a large diameter quick-fill fuel flap mounted at the very tail end of the car. At the front of the early cars was a cowled-in radiator that was distinctive of the hastily prepared item that adorned the EX 120 record car at Montlhéry. The top scuttle for the first time sported two humps directly in front of driver and passenger to deflect wind supposedly over the heads of the occupants. These humps were to become the hallmark of many an MG that was to follow over the ensuing 25 years. The instrumentation was to a high level and of very good quality and commensurate with the International Road Racing standards of the day. The final trappings of this racer were a gauze mesh windscreen, leather bonnet straps, and an external Brooklands type exhaust that terminated in a large fishtail. The complete package which very much looked the part, appealed instantly to the racing fraternity and was very conservatively priced at £295 being nearly £100 more that its standard sports car counterpart, the 'D type Midget. Nonetheless the car was considered to be very good value for such a highly specified vehicle and it sold very well, albeit in very small numbers, with only 44 being produced in total. Racing and competition successes that

ensued were many and various, probably the most notable was the first showing of thirteen 'C' types at the Brooklands Double Twelve Race in May 1931, where the cars secured the coveted team trophy and also one of the them winning the race in the hands of Lord March; 2nd to 5th place also going to 'C' types.

The beautiful Montlhéry Midget featured is a 1931 example and in unsupercharged form. This fairly rare MG is proudly owned by Colin Tieche and has been in his possession since the late sixties. The Midget is in Mark 3 configuration sporting a cross-flow cylinder head and horizontally mounted twin bronze carburettors and is one of 33 that are positively identified as remaining from the original 44 cars produced in 1931/32.

# 'C' TYPE MONTLHÉRY MIDGET

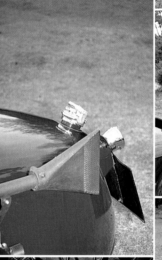

SPECIFICATION

Engine: 4 cylinder in line.

Capacity: 746 cc.

Bore & Stroke: 57mm x 73mm.

Valve operation: Single overhead camshaft driven through vertical dynamo.

Carburation: Various dependent on type of head.

Power Output: Various dependent on type of head, between 37.4 bhp unsupercharged and 52.5 bhp supercharged.

Gearbox: Four speed, ENV non-synchromesh.

Brakes: Cable operated. Early cars: Front 8" drum. Rear 8". Late cars: Front 10" drum. Rear 10".

Clutch: Twin dry plate.

Suspension: Semi elliptic front & rear in sliding trunnions.

Wheels: Centre lock wire spoke.

Wheelbase: 6' 9". Track: 3' 6" front and rear.

Number produced: 44

Cost new in 1931: £295.

# D Type Midget

The D Type Midget was in production from the latter part of 1931 to mid 1932 and was derived from the first of the MG Midget range, the M type that commenced production in late 1928. The M type was undoubtably the first of a long line of MGs that were to make the MG sports car so popular throughout the world and it is impossible to overestimate the importance of this little car In establishing the marque and associating it with affordable and exciting sports car motoring. The M type had its roots in the Morris camp and was loosely based on the Morris Minor that first appeared in early 1928. Cecil Kimber realised the importance of producing an MG based on the Morris which after all was hardly a surprising move as most of the forerunners were Morris derivatives.

Launched at the October 1928 Motor Show at Olympia, it was evident that the M type would be a success as there a full order book taken at the show and indeed the car sold very well for the ensuing three years. The car did not go into full production until early 1929 and used mainly Morris components with some modifications. The narrow two seater body and its exterior fittings were the main differences. The main reason for similarity with the Morris Minor counterpart was the fact that once the decision had been taken to produce the Midget there was tremendous pressure to get the car on show at Olympia and there was insufficient time to get individual components manufactured. Kimber had Carbodies of Coventry design the neat two seat boat-tailed fabric covered body and with a distinctive 'V' windscreen and louvred bonnet side panels, the car really looked the part. The overhead camshaft 847 cc engine was moderately tuned compared to the Morris Minor and it developed 20 bhp. At a later stage this was improved to 27 bhp but the engine designation of 8/33 as it appeared in the D type could not really be justified with the 8 signifying the horsepower and 33 indicating power output. A feature of the engine was the vertically mounted dynamo which carried the drive to the camshaft from the crank. There were benefits in mounting the dynamo in this way, the main one being the absorption of vibration coming from the camshaft drive with the heavy armature acting as a damper. A distinct disadvantage with this arrangement was that as time went by the top driveshaft seal in the cylinder head would fail and leak oil into the dynamo itself causing charging problems. The top coupling would then deposit generous amounts of oil all over the engine compartment as it rotated causing quite a mess!

Building on the success of the M Type, Cecil Kimber saw the potential of promoting the marque through competition and with the move to Abingdon in January 1930 and its improved production facilities and more space, he was able to convince Sir William Morris that the

time was right for MG to move into serious competition. Very soon Abingdon began to build the first real racing MGs. A team of five heavily modified M Type Midgets were produced to enter the Brooklands Double Twelve race where they triumphantly took the team prize. As a result 21 replica double twelve M Types were produced for sale to the public. Following the success at Brooklands and the ensuing publicity, it is fair to say that Sir William Morris could not fail to have been impressed and it is likely that he favoured further development of the racing side which resulted in the production of the C Type racing car. Derived

from the prototype EX 120 which was the first MG record breaker, it took the honour of the first 750cc car to exceed 100 mph, and was an out and out racing car. Only 44 of these were produced and Abingdon were ever mindful that the racers could only appeal to a very limited market and that the volume production cars, although benefiting greatly from the publicity and development point of view, they had to take precedence. Many of the racing features were emulated in the volume cars and this along with the racing successes certainly boosted sales. The C Type had many wins to its credit and on its first outing at the Brooklands Double Twelve race in May 1931 it not only one the race outright but the team prize also. Later on in the year, in supercharged form, the C Type won the Tourist Trophy outright which coincided nicely with the introduction of the D type at the London Motor Show in October.

With MG publicity riding high the D Type got off to a good start with plenty of initial interest. With a slightly longer wheelbase than the C Type but essentially the same chassis design with the main members underneath the rear axle and tubular cross members. The rear springs were mounted in sliding trunnions rather than shackles and the radiator was carried by the front. engine mounts rather than affixed directly to the chassis. Centre-lock Rudge Whitworth wire wheels were fitted and cable operated 8" drum brakes provided the stopping power. The 847cc engine and three speed gearbox with compact remote control unit were taken directly from the M Type as previously described. A rear mounted but enclosed 8 gallon fuel tank supplied the sin-

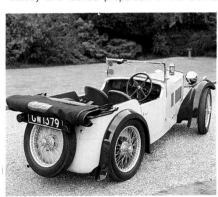

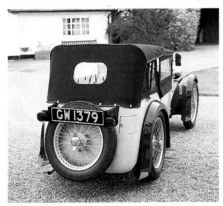

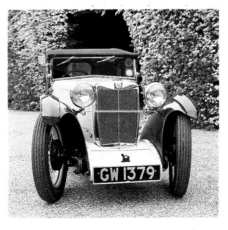

gle SU HV2 carburettor via an electric SU pump. The car looked somewhat short and stubby and lacked proportion in the bonnet length although many found the looks quite appealing. It was a heavy car and with only 27 bhp available to propel it, performance was not stunning. The bodywork options available were either closed or open 4 seaters, sadly no 2 seater sports were produced, possibly because the M Type was continued in production at the same time, albeit at a reduced price. The C Type was also still available retailing at £490 or £575 with supercharger, compared to £210 for the D Type open 4 seater, whilst the closed tourer D Type was on sale at £250. The M Type was reduced from £185 to £165 for the fabric bodied version whilst a new metal panelled option was available at £185. Launched at the same time and also based on the C Type chassis was the F Type which carried for the first time a new MG type name, the Magna. This car was greeted with slightly more enthusiasm as it sported a new 1271 cc 6 cylinder engine and an impressive 12/70 designation. The delightful 1932 D Type featured belongs to Kevin Horwood.

GW 1379

MG
OWNERS'
CLUB

# 'D' TYPE MIDGET

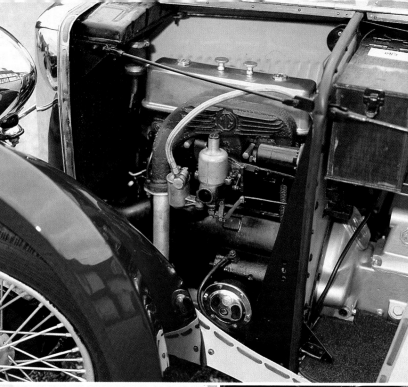

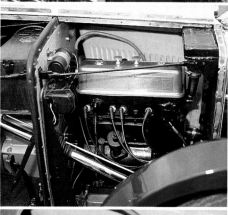

**SPECIFICATION**
Engine: 4 cylinder in line
Capacity: 847 cc
Bore & Stroke: 57mm x 83mm
Valve gear: Overhead camshaft driven through vertical dynamo
Carburation: Single SU HV2 type
Power output: 27 bhp @ 4,500 rpm
Gearbox: Manual three speed 'crash' box
Brakes: Mechanically operated cable system. 8" drums all round
Steering: Adamant box, worm drive
Clutch: Single dry plate
Suspension: half elliptic front and rear with sliding trunnions
Chassis: Underslung at rear, steel channel with tubular cross members, riveted construction
Wheels: Centre-lock Rudge Whitworth wire spoke
Wheelbase: Early cars 7' 0" late cars 7' 2"
Track: 3' 6" front and rear
Body types: Open and closed 4 seater
Numbers built late 1931-mid 1932: open 4 seater; 208 Salonette; 37 Chassis only; 5
Price New: open 4 seater; £210. Salonette; £250

In 1928 Cecil Kimber introduced an affordable sports car known as the M type Midget. It was simple, inexpensive yet proved highly successful in motor sport with its 8 horsepower 847cc Wolseley based engine. The Midget had comparable performance to the larger 14/40 and 18/80 models and at less than half the price of a 14/40 soon accounted for more than 50% of the total sales in the year following its introduction. The MG Car Company then had to move its operation to larger premises in Abingdon, this was eventually to become the world's largest sports car factory, with its distinctive brown and cream painted walls and many octagonal fitments.

With the huge success of the M Type Midget and the big price differential between it and the 18/80 range, it was fairly obvious that another model was needed to fill the gap after the ceasing of the old side valve Morris based cars. The Wolseley Hornet was introduced in 1930 with a 12 horsepower engine and was simply a stretched Morris Minor. Kimber was not overly impressed with this car and although he must have considered a 12 horse-power Midget, he was not tempted to put any ideas into production based on the Morris, besides the Abingdon design team were busy with plans for the Double Twelve version of the M type which was a far more important car that led the way for the C type Montlhéry Midget.

It was not until September 1931 that MG introduced its own 12 horsepower car designated the F type Magna. This was a six cylinder version of the D type which was launched at the same time and was a direct follow on from the C type. The two new chassis had sliding trunnion suspension and centre-lock wire wheels and both cars were offered with either a closed saloon type body or as an open 4 seater. The F type had a wheelbase of 7'10" whilst the D type had 7'0" wheelbase and shared the same axles, steering gear and brakes. Like the D type the F type had a rivetted steel chassis frame with an underslung rear axle. The extra length of the F type frame was to accommodate the six cylinder engine and the two rear seats. The engine was not a new design although Abingdon tried to pretend it was. The power unit was essentially a Wolseley Hornet engine with two extra cylinders tacked on and a lot of camouflaging sheet metal work around the block to disguise its origin. The capacity was 1271cc with a power output of 37bhp and both the camshaft and crankshaft ran in four main bearings, with the front bearing a ball race as with the Midget. The intermediate

bearings consisted of aluminium housings with white metalled bronze bushes, similar to those on the original Morris Oxford engines. The aluminium housings were clamped to the crankshaft and the whole unit was then fed through the front of the crankcase with the intermediate bearings clamped by long through bolts. The big ends consisted of white metal applied directly to the rods although some early engines utilised aluminium rods that required white metalled bronze bushes. The Camshaft was vertically driven and distinctly of M type parentage and the valve gear and porting was virtually the same as the M type as well. The drive was through a dry plate clutch and thence through a racing type ENV gearbox similar to that fitted on the C types with straight cut gears.

The F types generally lacked performance at the top end but there is no doubt that it was a genuine sports car and it looked the part. The car did sell well alongside the popular M type, the D type did not fair so well with only 250 being produced. The F type it was admitted was slightly underpowered for its size and weight and this was certainly emphasised when 4 adults were on board. The engine was undeniably smooth with plenty of torque from very low down in the rev range right the way through to maximum revs and a gearbox with ideal ratios gave the right combination for pleasurable driving. At the time of the 1932 Motor Show the specification of the F type was changed slightly with the addition of 12" brake drums and the fitting of extra water manifolding to aid cooling. These were seen as major improvements and a two seater version employing a J2 body was designated the F2 Magna and the new 4 seater version became known as the F3. It is worth noting though that having these additions does not automatically make the car an F2 or F3 as earlier F1s were fitted with these options by the factory as and when they became available. The F type certainly looked good in any of its various body styles which is one of the reasons why it enjoyed good sales, with the two and four seater option together with the salonette versions there were also variations built by some English coachbuilders. The beautiful 1932 F1 featured is owned by Barry Dean.

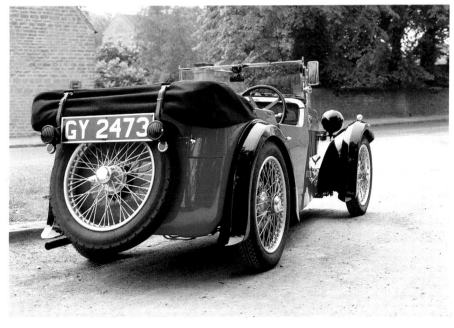

GY 2473

Specification
Engine: 6 cylinder in line.
Bore and Stroke: 57mm x 83mm.
Capacity: 1271cc.
Valve operation: Single overhead camshaft driven through vertical dynamo.
Carburation: Twin horizontal SUs.
Power output: 37.2 bhp @ 4,100 rpm.
Gearbox: Manual 4 speed non synchromesh.
Clutch: Single dry plate.
Brakes: Mechancially operated by Bowden cable. 8″ diameter drums round.
Suspension: Half elliptic front and rear with sliding trunnions.
Wheels: Centre lock wire spoke.
Wheelbase: 7′10″
Track: 3′6″ front and rear.
Length: 11′6.5″.
Width: 4′2″.
Weight: 19 cwts 1 qr.
Body types: 4 seat open and 4 seat salonette.
Max Speed: 72.58 mph.
Fuel consumption: Approx 26 mpg.
Number built: 1250.
Price new in 1932: Open sports: £250.
Closed Salonette: £289.

# F1 Magna Salonette

Launched at the latter end of 1931 in readiness for the 1932 model year were two entirely new MG models. "Motor" magazine dated September 8th 1931, billed the 12-70 h.p. Magna Six as the most interesting one, with the smaller 4 cylinder, 847 cc D type running a close second. Originally designated as the Magna Six, the car soon became known more commonly as the F type Magna and was first available in two versions either as an open four seater priced at £250 or as the featured car shows, a very attractive Foursome Coupe which sold for £289.

The reason for the introduction of the D and F type, stemmed from the need for some medium sized cars to fill the gap in the MG range between the highly successful M type Midget and at the other end of the spectrum, the large and sedate 18/80. Released in 1928, the M type was soon to capture the imagination of

Abingdon-on-Thames. This move noted the end of the Morris side valve engined cars with all efforts concentrated on increasing the production of the M type to meet public demand. Kimber turned his attentions towards Wolseley in need of a more modern power unit for the projected F Type. He focused on the Wolseley Hornet that had been introduced in 1930 and although he was not particularly impressed with the car itself he saw the potential in using a modified version of the 12 horsepower engine in an MG. The unit itself was not a new design although more up to date than any that Morris could offer. Abingdon tried to pretend that it was something new by camouflaging the exterior of the block with metal sheeting, disguising its origin but also adding to cooling problems. Often referred to as an M type engine with two cylinders 'tacked on' the 1271 cc unit had a meagre power output of 37.2 bhp at 4,100 rpm that resulted in disappointing performance. The Wolseley cylinder head was ported solely on the nearside with four inlet and five exhaust ports. A large cast iron inlet manifold sported twin carburettors whilst a finned exhaust manifold routed at the front of the engine followed a similar line to that of the M type Midget. A belt driven fan was fitted to aid engine cooling with the F type being the only overhead camshaft MG to have one fitted as standard. The vertically mounted dynamo formed the drive to the camshaft that was of distinct M type origin. The overall appearance of the engine was very neat, attributable no doubt in part to the aforementioned cladding. The engine was then mated to the hefty racing type four-speed ENV gearbox utilising straight-cut gears as used on the Montlhéry C type Midget.

No doubt due to feedback from owners of the first cars, the Abingdon engineers were soon working on extracting more power from the engine and in readiness for the 1932 Motor Show, a few other modifications were implemented. Higher compression, improved valve timing and larger carburettors contributed to a 27% increase in power whilst larger 12" brake drums and extra water manifoling to improve cooling, completed the package. These modifications were seen as major improvements and gave an added boost to sales. The range at this time was extended to include a two seater version designated the F2 which looked virtually the same as the J2 Midget but also had the benefit of previously mentioned 12" diameter brakes that had been developed principally for the racing C type Midget. The four seater Salonette was considered a well appointed car for its time and although somewhat cramped interior wise was quite refined. The distinctive glass sliding roof, often likened to 'a church window' provided good ventilation and some relief for claustrophobics! The bucket seating was described in brochures as 'close coupled' but as you would expect along with the rear seat and trim panels they were upholstered in quality leather. Accommodation for passenger luggage was somewhat restricted with the boot area totally swallowed up with the 6 gallon fuel tank. The hinged boot flap did have built in stays however that affixed to the lower trim rail in order to turn the flap into a horizontal luggage platform. In addition to the two seater, four seater and salonette versions, there were also variations on offer from specialist British coachbuilders of the day such as Jarvis, Styles, Abbey and Carlton to name but a few. The delightful 1932 Salonette featured, resplendent in its two tone apple green and black colour scheme, is a fine example of this rare model that has been restored with total originality in mind.

The owner is Timothy Edwards.

the public with its successes in motor sport and the fact that it offered meaningful performance at reasonable cost. This simple little sports car with its 8 horsepower, 847 cc Wolseley based engine had comparable performance to its larger stablemates, the 18/80 and 14/40, but at half the cost. It was so popular that it accounted for over 50% of production in the year following its introduction and was one of the reasons that the MG Car Company were forced to move to larger premises from their small mews garage in the centre of Oxford to former Pavlova Leather works at

The F types generally lacked performance, particularly with four adult passengers on board, nonetheless they were well received and sold steadily alongside the M type and D type. There is no doubt that it was a genuine sportscar that appealed in any of its various body options and with its long bonnet and raked radiator grille, certainly looked the part! With an undeniably smooth engine that had plenty of torque throughout the rev range and a gearbox that provided near perfect ratios, the combination afforded the right formula for pleasurable driving.

# F1 MAGNA SALONETTE

SPECIFICATION

Engine: 6 cylinder in line.

Bore & stroke: 57mm x 83mm.

Capacity: 1271 cc.

Valve operation: single overhead camshaft driven through vertical dynamo.

Carburation: Twin horizontal SU's.

Power output:
(early cars) 37.2 bhp @ 4,100 rpm
(later cars) 47 bhp @ 4,100 rpm.

Gearbox: ENV manual 4 speed non-synchromesh.

Clutch: Single dry plate.

Brakes: Mechanically operated 12" drum by Bowden cable.

Suspension: Half elliptic front and rear with sliding trunnions.

Wheels: Centre-lock Rudge Whitworth wire spoke.

Wheelbase: 7' 10".

Track: 3' 6" front and rear.

Number built: 390.

Price new in 1932: £289.

# F2 Magna

It was due in part to the tremendous success of the M type Midget that the MG Car Company had to move to larger premises in Abingdon from their small mews garage in the centre of Oxford. This move marked the end of

the old side valve cars and production was concentrated on the M type. This car was first introduced by Kimber in 1928 and although simple in its design it was a very affordable motor car and appealed to the growing band of motor sport enthusiasts as a vehicle they could compete with without great expense. The 8 horsepower 847cc Wolseley based engine gave comparable performance to the much larger 14/40 and 18/80 models at less than half the price of a 14/40 and very soon this model accounted for over 50% of the total sales in the year following its introduction. The move to Abingdon was effected in 1930 and the site chosen was next to the then disused Pavlova Leather factory and it was eventually to become the world's largest sportscar factory and the 'home' of MG. With its distinctive brown and cream painted walls and many octagonal fitments throughout, the Abingdon factory became a unique workplace for a workforce dedicated to producing sportscars that bore the famous octagon.

There was a large price differential between the M type and 18/80 range and it was obvious to Kimber that another model was needed to fill the gap after the ceasing of production of the old side valve Morris based cars. The Morris range itself was old fashioned and even they were not selling particularly well, Kimber turned his attentions to the Wolseley range of vehicles which were more up to date and in particular the Hornet which was introduced in 1930. This car had a 12 horsepower engine and although Kimber was not overly impressed at first with this car he must have considered the possibilities of a 12 horsepower Midget. No ideas were put into production at this stage because all efforts were concentrated on plans for the Double Twelve version of the M type Midget as this was considered far more important a project that ultimately led to the famous C type Montlhery Midget.

In September 1931 MG introduced its own 12 horsepower car designated the F type Magna. This was a six cylinder version of the D type

which was launched at the same time and was a direct follow on from the C type. Both cars had new chassis with sliding trunnion suspension and centre lock wire wheels and they were both available as either a closed saloon or as an open 4 seater. The F type had a wheelbase of 7' 10" whilst the D type had a 7' 0" wheelbase and shared the same axles, steering gear and brakes. Like the D type, the F type had a riveted steel chassis frame with an underslung rear axle. The extra length of the F type chassis was to accommodate the six cylinder engine and the two rear seats. The engine was not a new design although Abingdon tried to pretend that it was. It was very closely based on the Wolseley Hornet power unit and was essentially the same engine with two extra cylinders tacked on and a lot of sheet metal camouflage around the block to disguise its Wolseley origin. The capacity was 1271cc with a power output of 37bhp and both the camshaft and crankshaft ran in four main bearings, with the front bearing a ball race as with the Midget. The intermediate bearings consisted of aluminium housings with white metalled bronze bushes, similar to those used on the original Morris Oxford engines. The aluminium housings were clamped to the crankshaft and the whole unit was then fed through the front of the crankcase with the intermediate bearings clamped by long through bolts. The big ends consisted of white metal applied directly to the rods although some early engines utilised aluminium rods that required white metalled bronze bushes. The camshaft was vertically driven and distinctly of M type origin and the valve gear and porting was virtually the same as the M type as well. The drive was through a dry plate clutch and thence through a racing type ENV gearbox similar to that used on the C types with straight cut gears. The engine looked a very smart unit particularly with its steel cladding, however this did not aid the already overworked cooling system and this was fairly evident as it was the only model at the time to be

provided with a cooling fan as standard.

The F types generally lacked performance at the top end but there is no doubt that it was a genuine sportscar that also looked the part! The car sold very well alongside the very popular M type, the D type however did not fair so well with only 250 being produced. It was admitted that the F type was slightly underpowered for its size and weight and this was certainly emphasised when 4 adults were taken on board. The engine was undeniably smooth with plenty of torque from very low down in the rev range right the way through to maximum revs and the gearbox with near perfect ratios gave the right combination for pleasurable driving. At the time of the 1932 Motor Show the specification of the F type was changed slightly with the addition of 12" brake drums and the fitting of extra water manifolding to aid cooling. These modifications were seen as major improvements together with a higher compression ratio, different valve timing and larger carburettors, all in all the car was greatly improved. The engine modifications gave a 27% increase in power to 47 bhp. Later in 1932 saw the introduction of a two seater version known as the F2 Magna, it was very similar in appearance to the J2 and at the same time a 4 seat open tourer was announced designated the F3. The F type certainly looked good in any of its various body options which is why the car enjoyed good sales. In addition to the two seater, four seater and Salonette versions there were also variations on offer from some of the recognised English Coachbuilders of the day such as Jarvis, Styles, Abbey, Carlton, University Motors, Windover, Vanden Plas, Farnham, Wye and Meredith.

The F2 Magna featured has a very interesting

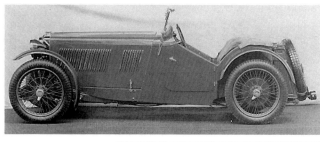

history, having once been owned by Royalty. The car as can be seen is totally original and has not been the subject of any restoration other than necessary maintenance and replacement of worn components. Owned by well known MG enthusiast Barry Bone, the car came into his possession in the mid sixties when he purchased it from Princess Chula who was living in England at the time. The F2 was given to Prince Bira as an 18th birthday present by his cousin Prince Chula in late 1932 and it is one of only 40 cars made. The car was the subject of considerable modification by Prince Bira and its 1271 cc engine has high compression pistons, balanced crankshaft, lightened flywheel, polished head and ports, stronger valve springs, larger 13/4" SU carburettor and straight through external exhaust.

# F2 Magna

SPECIFICATION
Engine: 6 cylinder in line
Bore and stroke: 57mm x 83mm
Capacity: 1271cc
Valve operation: Single overhead camshaft driven through vertical dynamo
Carburation: Single 1¾" SU
Power output (standard): 37.2bhp @ 4,100rpm
Gearbox: ENV 4 speed non synchromesh
Clutch: Single dry plate
Brakes: 12" drum brakes all round, mechanically operated by Bowden cable
Suspension: Half elliptic front and rear with sliding trunnions
Wheels: Centre lock wire spoke
Wheelbase: 7' 10"
Track and front and rear: 3' 6"
Chassis: Steel channel section, with tubular cross members
Number built: 40

# F2 Magna Jarvis bodied

In the autumn of 1929 the MG Car Company moved from their overcrowded Mews garage in the centre of Oxford to much larger premises that were formerly occupied by the Pavlova Leather Company at Abingdon-on-Thames. The move was due in part to the tremendous success of the M type Midget and it heralded the start of proper mass production of MGs. Although the purpose built garage in Edmund Road, Oxford had only been open some two years, conditions were becoming intolerable and the old Pavlova works although not ideal was now the new home of MG. Very soon the Abingdon works was to become the world's largest and most famous sports car factory. Cecil Kimber had the factory and offices decked out with a smart brown and cream colour scheme that became the company corporate colours, this together with many unusual fitments that bore the distinctive octagonal MG logo made the factory a unique place of work. At this time the now legendary slogan "Safety Fast" was adopted as a sales aid appearing in all literature and advertising.

The move to Abingdon marked the end of the old side valve cars and all efforts were concentrated on the high demand for the very affordable M type. Although quite simple in its

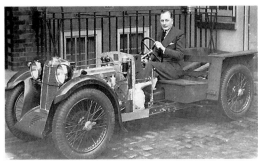

design the car appealed to the ever growing band of motor sports enthusiasts as a vehicle they could actively campaign in the sport without huge expense. With its 8 horsepower 847 cc Wolseley based engine the M type Midget had comparable performance to the larger and more expensive 14/40 and 18/80 models and priced at less than half the cost of a 14/40 the car sold particularly well and soon accounted for over 50% of the total production. With such a price differential it was very evident to Kimber that a new model was needed to bridge the price gap and after the demise of the old side valve Morris based cars he turned his attentions to the Wolseley camp. The range of Wolseleys was far more up to date and Kimber focused his attention on the Hornet that was introduced in 1930. This car had a 12 horsepower engine and although he was not overly impressed with the car as a whole he saw the potential that lay in the power unit. It was not until September 1931 that MG introduced its own 12 horsepower car, the F type Magna. The delay was due to all efforts being concentrated on the Double Twelve version of the M Type. This racing project was considered far more important and indeed led to the famous C type Montlhery Midget.

The F type was really a six cylinder version of the D type which was launched at the same time, both being derived from the aforementioned C type. The all new chassis was developed from the project codenamed EX 120 and was to set the standard for MG chassis design for many years to come. EX 120 was the first

of many MG record breaking cars and was the first 750 cc car to break the magic 100mph barrier, this was achieved in February 1931. Constructed of rivetted steel channel section with tubular cross members, the chassis was underslung the rear axle and carried sliding trunnion suspension and centre lock wire wheel axles. Both the D type and F type were available as closed saloons or open sports, however the D type open sports was a four seater only in common with the F1 Magna, whilst the F2 Magna was a 2 seater sports. The F type had a wheelbase of 7' 10" whilst the D type was 7' 0" and they both shared the same axles, steering gear and brakes. The extra length of the F type chassis was in the main to accommodate the six cylinder engine. As previously described the engine was not a new design although Abingdon engineers tried to pretend that it was. It was very closely based on the Wolseley Hornet power unit and was essentially the same engine with two extra cylinders tacked on and a lot of sheet metal camouflaging around the block to disguise its Wolseley origins. The capacity was 1271 cc with a power output of 37 bhp and both the camshaft and crankshaft ran in four main bearings with the camshaft vertically driven through the dynamo which was distinctly of M type origin. The drive was trough a dry plate clutch and thence through a racing type ENV gearbox similar to that used on the C types with straight cut gears. The engine looked particularly smart with its cladding but this did not aid the already overworked cooling system and this was evidenced by the fact that it was the only model at the time to be fitted with a cooling fan as standard.

The F types generally lacked performance at the top end but there is no doubt that it was a genuine sportscar that certainly looked the part and it sold very well alongside the ever popular M type. It was acknowledged that the F types were underpowered for their size and weight and this was particularly emphasised when four adults were taken on board. However the engine was undeniably smooth with plenty of torque from well down in the rev range right the way through to maximum revs and the gearbox with near perfect ratios gave the right combi-

nation for pleasurable driving. In 1932 at the London Motor Show the specification for the F types was changed for the better with the addition of 12" brake drums and extra manifolding to aid cooling. At the same time the valve timing was altered and larger carburettors were fitted that contributed to a 27% increase in power to 47 bhp giving improved performance. The F2 Magna was launched at this time employing a J2 body and the new 4 seater version became known as the F3. It is worth noting that having the above additions did not necessarily make the car an F2 or F3 as earlier F1 s were fitted with these options by the factory as and when they became available. The F type certainly looked good in any of its body options and is one of the reasons why the cars enjoyed good sales. In addition to the two seater four seater and Salonette there were also on offer coachbuilt variations from such companies as Jarvis, Styles, Abbey, Carlton University Motors, Windover, Vanden Plas, Farnham, Wye and lastly Meredith.

One such coachbuilt example is featured and is the 1932 Jarvis bodied F type Magna belonging to William Opie. The firm of Jarvis and Son was originally established in Wimbledon in 1867 and had made its name in the construction of fine horse carriages. In the late 20's their skills were turned to the fabrication of special bodies for road and racing cars which were to their own design. Some of their notable customers included Sir Malcolm Campbell and Wolf Barnato of Bentley renown. It was not until the early 1930's that an association with MG was formed. One of the Jarvis Directors, Jimmy Palmes was very friendly with George Eyston, having shared a room at Cambridge University and it was no surprise that Eyston joined the board of Directors at Jarvis for what was to be a long and most beneficial association. The MG factory had already designed EX 120 as previously mentioned in which Eyston successfully broke the 100 mph barrier and although Jarvis did not get involved with this project the successor to EX 120, EX127 better known as the 'Magic Midget' was designed and constructed at Jarvis's Wimbledon premises. This car was far more streamlined than EX 120 and benefitted from the earlier development work enabling it to take the record for two miles per minute in the 750cc class. Jarvis had carried a Morris franchise since 1925 for the supply of new vehicles and with the record breakers came the agency for MG alongside its MOWOG partners Wolseley and latterly Riley. Their first coachbuilt MG was based of the M type and was a deluxe version of superior quality. The car carried exclusive approval by the MG Car Company and sold for £225 which was considerably more than the £165 that the standard boat tailed M type sold for.

There was a healthy demand for this 'up market' car and following in its success was the Jarvis F type Magna. Its main distinguishing features were the higher sill line and the shape of the doors that were curved outwards at the bottom of the leading edge to give ease of access to the driver and passenger enabling them to swing in their legs comfortably. The windscreen pillar supports are also unique and a source of reference. At the rear the spare wheel carrier retaining spinner and the petrol tank arrangements were exclusive to the model and another identifying feature. The Jarvis F Type was on sale at £289 as opposed to the Abingdon standard car at £250.

# Jarvis bodied F Type Magna

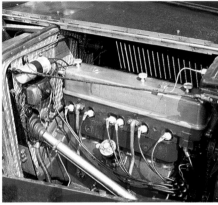

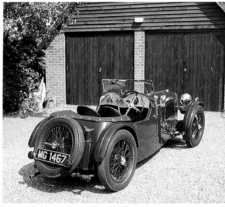

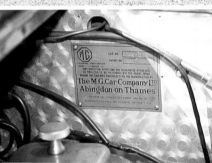

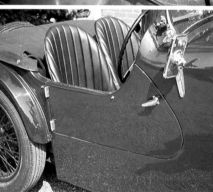

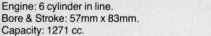

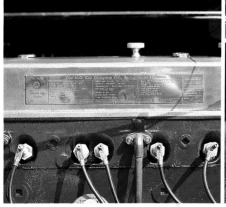

**SPECIFICATION**

Engine: 6 cylinder in line.

Bore & Stroke: 57mm x 83mm.

Capacity: 1271 cc.

Valve operation: Single overhead camshaft driven through vertical dynamo.

Carburation: Twin horizontal SU's OM type.

Power Output: 37.2 bhp @ 4,100 rpm.

Gearbox: ENV 4 speed non-synchromesh.

Clutch: Single dry plate.

Brakes: Mechanically operated by Bowden cable, 10" drums.

Suspension: Half elliptic front and rear with sliding trunnions

Wheels: Centre lock Rudge wire spoke.

Wheelbase: 7' 10".

Track: 3' 6' front and rear.

Numbers Built: F1 tourer; 565. F1 salonette;370. F2; 40. F3 tourer; 67. F3 salonette; 20. Chassis only; 188 which comprise approx 27 Jarvis bodied cars.

The J series of MG Midgets was to be a refinement of the C and D Type forerunners, announced in 1932 at the Motor Show a whole new series of cars made their debut. The J1 was offered with 4 seater open or closed bodywork and the J2 was strictly a two seater sports and the racing variants, the J3 and J4 although launched to the public, were not to go into production until early 1933. The J2 was very well received by the motoring public and was soon to become one of the classic sports cars of the era, it was within reach of many enthusiasts, sensibly priced at £199 10s it gave outstanding performance and value for money. The J1 was sold for £220 with a Salonette version at £255. The cars were based on the successful design of the C type or Montlhery Midget as it had become known, which was in itself a direct derivative of the M type Midget. The J1 was a pretty looking car and was a practical 4 seater sports returning reasonable performance from its race developed 847cc engine. This was based on the power unit used in the M type and was Wolseley derived.

Motor magazine gave extensive editorial to the new range of Midgets leading with a banner headline '80mph MG Midget for under £200'. This statement, although true, caused considerable embarrassment later on for Cecil Kimber. He had instructed Reg Jackson, one of his top development engineers to ensure that all the press cars were capable of at least 80mph. This he duly did and reports in the press gave great prominence to this with S C H Davis of Autocar reporting that he had achieved 82mph on road test. Several days later the two main bearing crankshaft broke on this particular car and the factory had to lower the compression ratio for the start of the production run. The J2 was then dogged with complaints from owners bemoaning the fact that their cars would not perform as Autocar said they would!

The chassis layout of the J1 and J2 followed that of the C type incorporating virtually straight side members passing under the rear axle with tubular cross supports. The suspension was half elliptic all round with sliding trunnions. Cable operated brakes utilising 8" finned drum brakes were quite effective for the size of car. The racing type hand brake lever was mounted on a shaft linked to the foot pedal and four cables which allowed easy adjustment of the brakes were linked into each wheel. Friction type Hartford shock absorbers were fitted front and rear with the latter being mounted transversely. The chassis was lubricated by a Tecalemit central greasing system with the grease nipples neatly grouped each side of the lower bulkhead wall. Other features of the J series included a twelve volt Rotax lighting and starting system fed from a vertically mounted dynamo. Rudge Whitworth cen-

tre lock wire wheels and Marles steering gear that was adjustable for rake completed the package .

The J1 and J2 set the fashion in MG cars for many years to come with the J2 displaying a classic humped scuttle and low cut away doors. The J1 was a little more sedate with a flatter topped scuttle incorporating a less sporting but nonetheless highly functional dashboard. This had an enclosed glovebox on the near side with a dummy one for symmetry on the off side on which was mounted the horn push and dip switch. The long bonnet seemed out of proportion with the rest of the car, but this concealed not only the engine and gearbox, but the foot controls and the legs of the driver and passenger as well! On lifting the bonnet is seemed odd to peer into the footwell and cockpit from the engine compartment, but this design had its advantages for ease of maintenance and it also kept the passenger compartment reasonably warm from the heat generated by the engine. The tail of both the J1 and J2 was relatively short and stubby with the J2 only extended by the externally mounted 12 gallon slab tank and carrier mounted spare wheel. The J1 had a bulbous rear end with only a 6 gallon tank concealed behind the rear seat. A neat lockable hinged fuel flap was incorporated on the nearside rear corner of the car. Other differences on the J1 were the side shields faired into the cycle type front wings, giving greater protection from road dirt and water.

Power came from the well tried 847cc engine as used on the successful M type which was originally derived from the Wolseley Hornet. With an 8 port crossflow cylinder head and twin carburettors, this unit produced a healthy 36 bhp at 5,500 rpm, however as previously

described with only a two main bearing crankshaft, revving the engine to its maximum, soon produced premature failure of the flimsy crankshaft. The vertically mounted dynamo was driven off the front end of the crankshaft, with its armature forming part of the overhead camshaft drive. This particular design was a weak point on these engines with the seals leaking oil onto the dynamo causing embarrassing flat batteries. The gearbox now sported four forward speeds unlike the earlier three speed gearboxes of the M and D types; it also had a neat remote control gearchange enclosed in an alloy casing, bringing the gear lever conveniently to the drivers hand. The top two ratios were close, giving a good high speed range, whilst first and second gears were sufficiently low for either trials work or the unexpected very steep hill, with a fair step between second and third gear. A single plate dry clutch transferred the power via a Hardy Spicer propshaft to the three quarter floating rear axle.

Later on in 1932 the J3 and J4 became available. The J3 being a supercharged version of the J2 and it had a 746cc version of the C type engine, in every other respect it was the same as the J2 but with superior performance if suitable sparking plugs were available! The J4 was the model Abingdon offered specifically for racing, this likewise was basically a J2 but with different steering gear and larger 12" drum brakes as found on the Magna. All the racing extras were evident such as quick fill

caps on the radiator and fuel tank, leather bonnet straps, side exit fishtailed exhaust and with safety in mind no doors were fitted necessitating a leap over the side of the car to get into the driving seat. The J4 was a fast car with several runs of over 100 mph being recorded at Brooklands and there is no doubt that through continuous development of the J series from the J1 to the J4 that it captured the imagination of the sportscar enthusiast. Despite adverse criticism of fuel starvation problems on early J2s and the previously mentioned dynamo oil leaks problems, careful maintenance gave good reliable service and the cars were in fact able to withstand far more hard use than any other comparable competitor at the time. The 1933 J1 featured is owned by George Baxter.

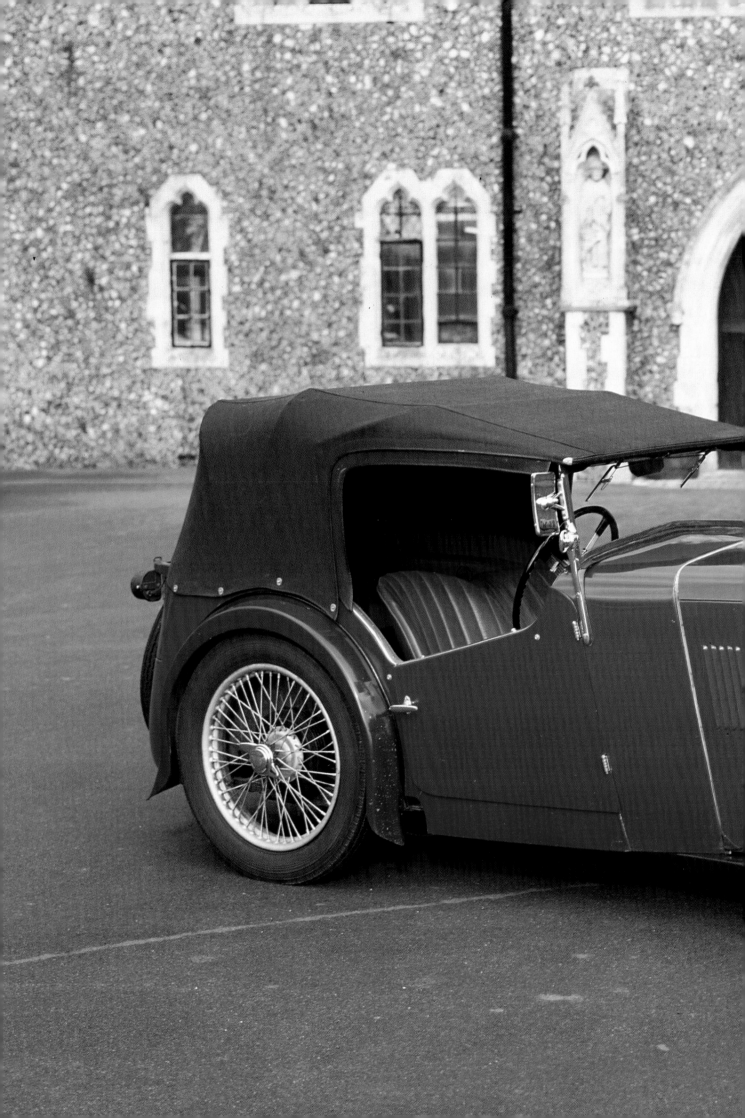

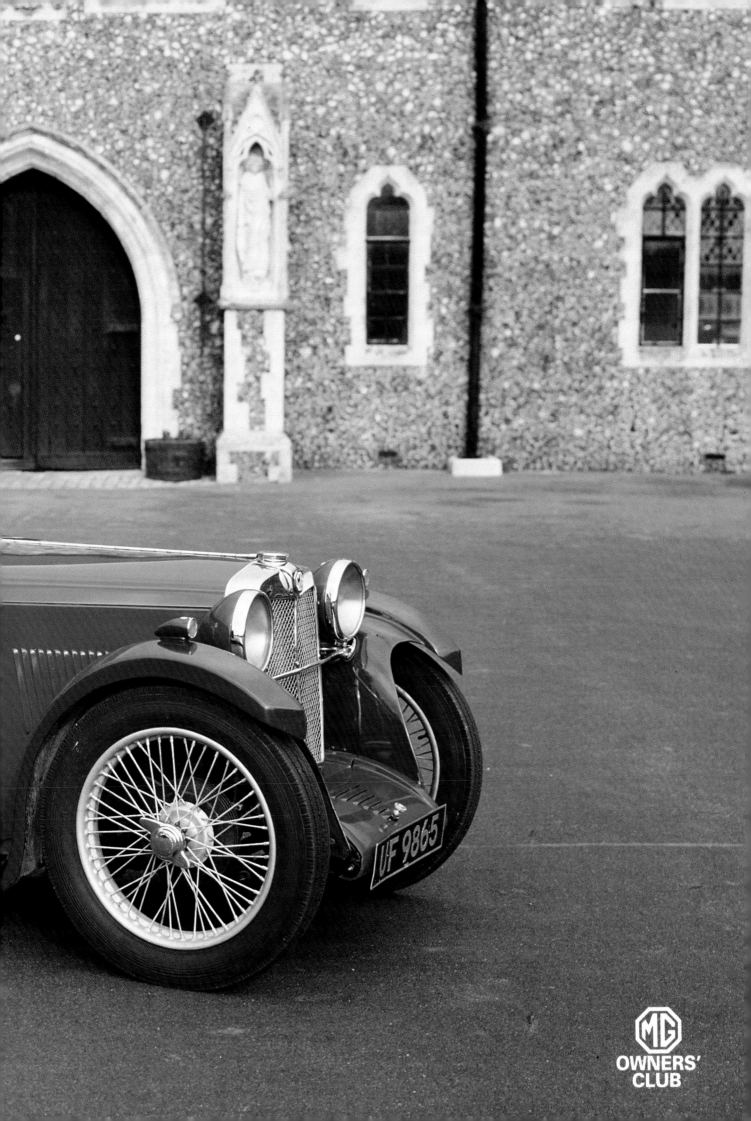

# J1 Midget

SPECIFICATION:
Engine: In line, water cooled.
Number of cylinders: 4
Bore and Stroke: 57mm x 83mm
Capacity: 847cc
Valve operation: Overhead Camshaft, driven through vertical dynamo.
Carburation: Twin semi-downdraught SUs
Compression Ratio: 6.2:1
Power output: 36 bhp @ 5,500 rpm
Clutch: Single dry plate
Transmission: Manual 'crash' 4 forward speeds and reverse.
Chassis: Twin side frame with tubular cross members.
Wheelbase: 7' 2"
Track: 3' 6" front and rear.
Suspension: Front: half elliptic springs beam axle.
Rear: half elliptic springs, live axle.
Brakes: 8" drum cable operated.
Tyres: 27 x 4
Wheels: Centre lock Rudge Whitworth wire spoke.
Performance: Maximum speed 75 mph.
Fuel consumption: approx 35 mpg
Acceleration: 0-60 mph approx 15 secs.
Number built mid 1932 to early 1934: 380
Cost new in 1932: £255.

# J2 Midget

Announced in August 1932 the J2 Midget was outstanding value for just £199 10s and was within the reach of many enthusiasts of the era. It was based on the successful design of the C type or Montlhéry Midget as it was better known, a direct derivative of the M type. From

the outset the car represented everything that was right in basic sports car design, incorporating such things as a large rear mounted slab type petrol tank with a huge fast fill petrol cap, fold flat windscreen with optional aero screens, centre lock wire wheels, remote control gear change and a spring spoked flat steering wheel. A temperature gauge, eight day electric clock, leather securing strap over the bonnet and protective mesh grilles for the headlamps and radiator completed the package of extras for an additional cost of £12 12s.

The chassis layout followed that of the C type incorporating virtually straight side members passing under the rear axle with tubular cross supports. The suspension was half elliptic all round on sliding trunnions. Cable operated brakes utilising 8 inch drums were quite effective for the size of car. The hand brake lever was mounted on a shaft linked to the foot pedal and four cables which allowed easy adjustment of the brakes. Friction type Hartford shock absorbers were fitted front and rear, with the latter being mounted transversely. The chassis was lubricated by a Tecalemit central greasing system, with the grease nipples neatly grouped on the back of the bulkhead wall. Other features of the chassis included a 12 volt Rotax lighting and starting system. Rudge Whitworth wire wheels and Marles steering gear which was adjustable for rake. Whereas its forerunner the J1 was offered with 4 seater open or closed bodywork, the J2 was strictly a 2 seater and set the fashion in MG

sports cars for many years to come. With its classic 'two humped' scuttle and low 'cut away' doors the car was a masterpiece of simple, functional race bred design and is today considered by many to be one of the classic sports cars of all time. The long bonnet which seems out of proportion to the rest of the car conceals not only the engine but gearbox, foot controls and the legs of the driver or passenger! On lifting the bonnet it seems odd by todays standards to peer into the footwell and cockpit from the engine compartment, but this design had its advantages for ease of maintenance. The tail of the car was short and stubby only extended by the 12 gallon slab tank and the strapped-on spare wheel. Initially the car was produced with cycle-type front and rear wings, to be replaced a year later with long swept wings.

Power came from the well tried 847cc engine as used on the successful M type which was originally derived from a Wolseley unit with an eight port crossflow cylinder head and twin SU carburettors, this unit produced a healthy 36 bhp at 5500 rpm. though with only a two main bearing crankshaft, revving the engine to its maximum soon produced premature failure of the flimsy crankshaft. A vertically mounted dynamo was driven off the front end of the crankshaft, with its armature forming part of the overhead camshaft drive. This particular design was a weak point on these engines with seals leaking oil into the dynamo, causing embarrassing flat batteries.

The gearbox now sported four forward speeds unlike the earlier three speed gearboxes of the M and D types; It also had a neat remote gearchange enclosed in an alloy casting, bringing the gear lever very conveniently to the driver's hand. The top two ratios were close,

giving a good high speed range, whilst first and second gears were sufficiently low for either trials work or the unexpected very steep hill, with a fair step between second and third. A single plate dry clutch transfers the power via a Hardy Spicer prop shaft to the three-quarter floating rear axle.

A supercharged version of the J2 was produced known as the J3 and had a 750cc unit, in every other respect it was the same as a J2 but with superior performance. The racing variant of the J series was called the J4, this also was basically the same as the J, but with different steering gear and larger 12" drum brakes as found on the Magnas. The J4 was a fast car with several runs of over 100 mph being recorded at Brooklands and there is no doubt that through the continuous development of the J type from the J1 to the J4, it captured the imagination of the sportscar enthusiast. Despite adverse criticism of fuel starvation problems on early J2's and the dynamo oil leak problems mentioned before, careful maintenance gave good reliable service and the cars were in fact able to withstand far more hard use than any other comparable competitor at the time. The beautiful J2 featured is owned by David Diplock.

# J2

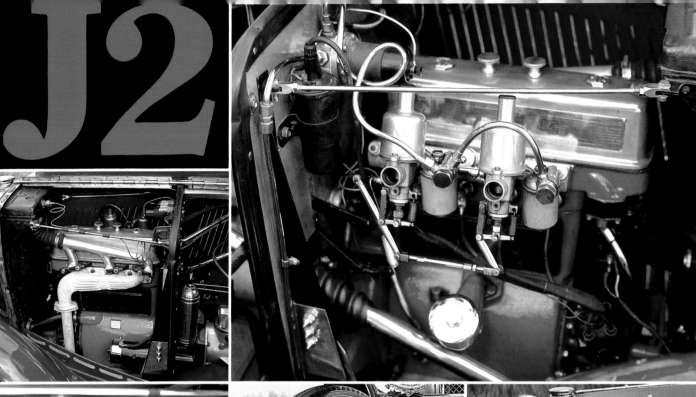

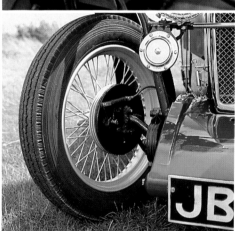

**Specification:**

Engine:

Type: In line, water cooled.

No. of cylinders: 4

Bore/Stroke: 57mm x 83mm.

Capacity: 847cc

Valve Operation: Overhead Camshaft, driven through vertical dynamo.

Carburation: Twin semi downdraught SU.

Compression ratio: 6.2:1.

Power output: 36 bhp at 5500 rpm.

Drive Train:

Clutch: Single dry plate.

Transmission: Manual 'crash' 4 forward speeds and reverse.

Chassis:

Frame: Twin side members, tubular cross members.

Wheelbase: 7' 2''

Track: 3' 6'' front and rear.

Suspension: Front: half elliptic springs, beam axle. Rear: half elliptic springs, live axle.

Lenth: 10' 4''

Width: 4' 3''

Height: 4' 5''

Brakes: 8'' drums cable operated

Tyre size: 277'' x 4''

Wheels: Centre lock, detachable wire wheels.

Performance:

Maximum Speed: 80 mph

Fuel consumption: approx 35 mpg

Acceleration: 0-50 mph; 15 secs.

Number built: Mid 1932 to early 1934; 2083

Cost new in 1932: £199 10s.

# J3 Midget

It was in August 1932 that the J series Midgets were announced with Cecil Kimber too impatient to wait for the London Motor Show in October of that year. The whole Midget range was in need of rationalisation and this was certainly achieved with the new Midgets. There were 4 models announced, J1, J2, J3 and J4 with only the J1 and J2 available initially. With the J2 selling for just £199.10s and the J1 for marginally more the cars were within the reach of many enthusiasts of the era. The J1 was offered with 4 seater open or closed bodywork whilst the J2 was strictly a two seater sports car. The J3 and J4 variants, although announced, did not appear until mid 1933 and were specifically aimed at the racing fraternity. The new range replaced the M, C and D type Midgets which were by now becoming outdated and in the case of the D type and M type lacking power with their 27 bhp engines.

The J type chassis was derived from the C and D types but the power unit and gearbox was quite different, with the engine sporting an eight port cross-flow cylinder head, that increased output to 36 bhp with the capacity of 847cc but still retaining a two main bearing crankshaft. The old three speed gearbox with roots in the Morris Minor family and used in the D and M type, gave way to a new four speed gearbox with remote control gear lever. Most important of all was the revised body styling which was to become the yardstick for most MG models that were to follow over the next twenty years or so, the basic design was also copied by other sports car manufacturers of the time. The design showed its race bred origin with humped scuttles and deep cutaway doors and a large externally mounted slab type fuel tank which also had the spare wheel mounted on it. The two seat J2 was soon to be acknowledged as one of the classic sports cars of all time and a car that was both functional, economical and blessed with quite lively performance. The J2 appeared initially with cycle wings but a year later the car sported long swept wings which to many was a retrograde step, however it seemed that MG had a recipe for a design that was to change little through the different models until 1955.

The J3 was essentially a supercharged J2 but had a 746cc engine similar to the earlier C type and utilising the bore and stroke of the race prepared MGs but without a counterbalanced crankshaft. This size of engine was retained for all the racing Midgets until the arrival of the PB Midget. The bodywork was very similar to the J2 and although the car was intended for

road use, many found their way into competition achieving good results in rallies and trials. The J3 was intended as an affordable yet fast sports tourer but its fine turn of speed made it eminently suitable for the enthusiast who wished to race or enter trials at the weekend. The car was endowed with comfortable seating, sensible suspension and weather equipment to make long distance touring a pleasure, whilst the out and out racer was the J4 which was similar in profile to the J2 and J3 but that is where the similarity ended. The body was door-less and the power unit was in full racing specification and carried all the latest developments. This was a very fast car indeed and certainly not for the fainthearted, in fact there were very few drivers who could handle the car properly. Abingdon seemed to be pushing the boundaries of chassis design to the limit with the J4 by putting such a powerful engine within. Large 12" brake drums all round went some way to help arrest the car from the high speeds it was capable of and a new type of split track rod end steering was employed which alleviated the common problem of 'kickback' associated with normal systems. This split link sys-

tem was adopted on all MG racing cars in 1933/34 including the K series cars. The J4 was supercharged and there was listed an unsupercharged version, designated J5, however, this never went into production, probably because of the limited interest shown at the time in the J4. There were in fact, only nine J4's produced, with cost probably being a limited factor as it had a selling price of £495. As already described the J4 was a very fast car with several runs of over 100 mph being recorded at Brooklands. There is no doubt that through continuous development of the J type from J1 to J4 it captured the imagination of the true sports car enthusiast.

Motoring journals of the time gave the cars very good reviews and this may be due in part to some 'doctoring' of the press cars by the Abingdon engineers. Speeds of over 80 mph were often obtained by journalists, but strangely the standard production cars were doing well if they achieved 70 mph! This prompted complaints by owners to the Abingdon Service Department about the performance of their cars. The J3 featured belongs to Terry Holden and was first registered in April 1933 bearing chassis number J3765. The car was used extensively by the original owner for trials and racing during the period 1933-34 with several appearances at Brooklands racetrack. Terry has built up a well documented history of the car which includes many period photographs of the car in competition. He also has letters written by the original owner that describe his exploits with the car and explain various modifications. Reference is made to the fact that the J3 would achieve 88 mph in 3rd, 106 mph in top and take a mere 9.5 seconds to reach 50 mph, no mean feat for a 746 cc motor car! Departures from the standard specification on Terry's J3 include a Centric 240 Supercharger fed by a 1.75" SU carburettor. It is also believed that it is the only J3 to be fitted with 12" brakes by the factory.

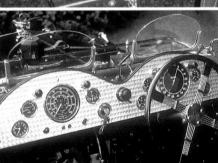

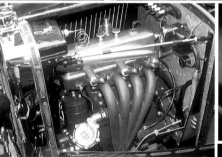

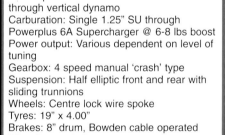

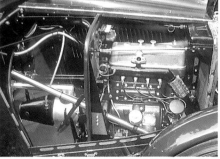

SPECIFICATION
Engine
No of cylinders: 4 in line
Bore & stroke: 57mm x 73mm
Capacity: 746cc
Valve operation: Overhead camshaft driven through vertical dynamo
Carburation: Single 1.25" SU through Powerplus 6A Supercharger @ 6-8 lbs boost
Power output: Various dependent on level of tuning
Gearbox: 4 speed manual 'crash' type
Suspension: Half elliptic front and rear with sliding trunnions
Wheels: Centre lock wire spoke
Tyres: 19" x 4.00"
Brakes: 8" drum, Bowden cable operated
Wheelbase: 7' 2"
Track: 3' 6" front and rear
Fuel tank capacity: 11 gallons
Numbers produced: 1932-34: J1:379, J2:2061, J3:22, J4:9, chassis only:23.
Body types: J1 open and closed 4 seater, J2,J3 and J4 open 2 seater only.
Price new: £299 10s 0d

# J4 Midget

The J4 Midget was made available to the MG fraternity in the spring of 1933 and this car along with the J3 completed the J series range. The J series were first announced in August 1932 prior to the Motor Show of that year with Cecil Kimber too impatient to wait for the annual gathering of the worlds motor manufacturers displaying their new models. The whole Midget range was in need of rationalisation and this was most certainly achieved with the J types. With only the J1 and J2 available initially, the J1 carried four seat open and closed bodies, whilst the J2 was the open two seater sports version. Some 9 months later the J3 and J4 versions followed with the J3 basically being a supercharged J2 and the J4 the out and out racing car.

This new range replaced the M, C and D type Midgets which were by now becoming outdated. It was the M type that started the Midget series in 1929 and from this model evolved the C type Montlhéry Midget which was the first MG produced specifically for racing. Each racing model produced by the MG Car Company had to be economically priced and yet cover its limited production run costs. This was achieved by commonality of parts with the sports cars that were marketed alongside. In the case of the C type, its sports counterpart was the D type which carried either a four seat open or closed salonette body. The three models described were all being produced together as a complete range. At the same time however a new series of light six cylinder cars was introduced commencing with the F type Magna. This car, although looking quite different to the rest of the current range was in fact a good illustration of the use of common components. Excluding the engine which was really M type with two extra cylinders added, the F type was made up mainly from parts used in the C and D types.

The J type chassis was derived from the C and D types but the power unit and gearbox was quite different with the engine sporting an eight port cross-flow cylinder head that increased output to 36bhp with a capacity of 847cc but still retaining a two main bearing crankshaft. The old three speed gearbox with roots in the Morris Minor family and used in the D and M type gave way to a new four speed gearbox with remote control gear lever. Most important of all was the revised body styling which was to become the yardstick for most MG models that were to follow over the next twenty years

or so, the basic design was also copied by other sports car manufacturers of the time. The design showed its race bred origin with humped scuttles and deep cutaway doors and a large externally mounted slab type fuel tank which also had the spare wheel mounted on it The two seat J2 was soon to be acknowledged as one of the classic sports cars of all time and a car that was both functional, economical and blessed with quite lively performance. The J2 appeared initially with cycle wings but a year later the car sported long swept wings which to many was a retrograde step, however it seemed that MG had a recipe for a design that was to change little through the different models until 1955.

The J3 was essentially a supercharged J2 but had a 750 cc engine similar to the earlier C type and utilising the bore and stroke of the race prepared MGs but without a counterbalanced crankshaft. This size of engine was retained for all the racing Midgets until the arrival of the PB Midget. The bodywork was very similar to the J2 and was intended for road use although many found their way into competition achieving good results in rallies and trials.

The racing J4 was produced as a replacement for the C type which had been proven too fast for its (and the drivers) own good. Supercharging the C type made it an extremely quick car but limitations of the braking system caused its demise. There was every intention of making the J4 racer go even faster and to date all the small MGs had carried 8" brake drums. As a result new brake gear had to be developed for the J4 but price constraints would not allow for producing anything special for it. As it happened, the F type Magna replacement, the 6 cylinder L type, afforded the opportunity for utilising its 12" drum brake system. So with L type brakes, J2 chassis frame and axles, and C type gearbox the J4 was born. The body was door-less and the power unit was in full racing specification and carried all the latest developments. This was a very fast car indeed and certainly not for the faint hearted, in fact there were very few drivers who could handle

the car properly. Abingdon seemed to be pushing the boundaries of chassis design to the limit with the J4 by putting such a powerful engine within. The large 12" brake drums all round went some way to help arrest the car from the high speeds it was capable of and a new type of split track rod end steering was employed which alleviated the common problem of 'kickback' associated with normal systems. This split link system was adopted on all MG racing cars in 1933/34 including the K series cars. The J4 was supercharged and there was listed an unsupercharged version, designated J5, however this never went into production, probably because of the limited interest shown at the time in the J4.

There were in fact only nine J4s produced with cost probably being a limiting factor as it had selling price of £495. As already described the J4 was a very fast car with several runs of over 100 mph being recorded at Brooklands. There is no doubt that through continuous development of the J type from J1 to J4 it captured the imagination of the true sports car enthusiast. The magnificent J4 featured belongs to Colin Teiche who is an authority on the Triple-M pre-war MGs. This famous 1933 MG is the ex-Hugh Hamilton car and bearing chassis number J4002 was the first J4 to he built. Hugh was a great exponent of the marque and a driver who met with considerable success competing with the Midget all over Europe, and in fact took the car to 2nd place behind Nuvolari at the RAC International T.T. Race in 1933.

# J4

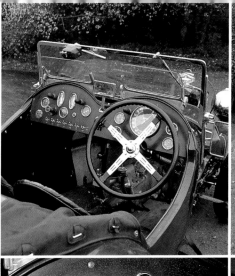

## SPECIFICATION

Engine No of cylinders: 4

Bore & stroke: 57mm x 73mm

Capacity: 746cc Valve Operation: Overhead camshaft driven through vertical dynamo.

Carburation: Single SU with various Powerplus Superchargers.

Power output: 72.3 bhp at 6000 rpm.

Clutch: Dry plate clutch

Gearbox: 4 Speed manual ENV 'crash' type.

Suspension: half elliptic front and rear with sliding trunnions.

Wheels: Centre lock wire spoke. Brakes: 10″ drum, Bowden cable operated.

Wheelbase: 7′ 2″

Track: 3′ 6″ front and rear.

Numbers produced 1932-34; J1:379, J2:2061, J3:22, J4:9, chassis only: 23

# K1 Magnette

The MG model range was already quite varied in the early thirties, when at the 1932 Motor Show several more interesting models were introduced. The very popular Magna range of MGs was complimented by the addition of what was to be known as the K Series Magnettes. The cars followed on in logical sequence from the successful J types with the K1 and K2 utilising the now familiar and well established conventional MG chassis layout. The racing K3 although announced at the Motor Show did not in fact appear until early 1933 and then only as a prototype. The idea behind the K series cars was principally to assist Cecil Kimber with his desire to carry his racing activities into Class G (1100cc), this class fell midway between the 847cc Midgets and the 1271cc Magnas. It was difficult for Kimber to justify producing a racing model on its own at that time hence the K1 and K2 models formed the basis for the important new racing model.

The MG model range was particularly confusing at this time and the various permutations that were to be available on the K Magnette series did nothing but add to the confusion. There were to be three different chassis (K1, K2 and K3), four different engines (KA, KB, KD and K3) and three different gearboxes all being fitted into five different body variations. With such small quantities of each model being produced it was little wonder that no two cars seemed alike! All four engine units retained the 57mm bore of earlier engines but had a stroke of 71 mm to give a cubic capacity of 1087cc giving Kimber his entry into Class G for racing and record breaking purposes.

The K types were available at first in two chassis lengths with the K1 having a wheelbase of 9'0" and the K2 being 7'10" with a track of 4'0" in each case. 13" cable operated drum brakes all round provided the stopping power and although the engines were only 1087cc they did produce more power than their larger engined predecessors, the Magnas. Sporting a cross flow head and stronger crankshaft, the engine fitted initially was known as the KA and was based closely on the Wolseley Hornet unit. This proved underpowered for the long wheelbase K1 and the short wheelbase K2, so very shortly after the two models had gone into production, a more powerful KB type engine was made available. These engines were fitted into the open tourers as they were deemed more worthy of the extra power, whilst the more sedate saloons retained the less powerful KA engine. The KA engine had a special camshaft which gave slower timing, thus allowing a far slower tickover speed. This was essential for the satisfactory functioning of the pre-selector gearboxes. Idle speeds needed to be below 500rpm to avoid the car 'creeping' when the brakes were released. The K1 was offered either as a very attractive pillarless 4 door, four seater saloon or slightly later as an open four seater sports. This version was available either with a four speed 'crash' gearbox or with a Wilson pre-selector transmission. The K2 was strictly a two seater sports and the chassis and body were essentially a widened version of the J2 with the classic cutaway doors and sweeping front wings.

The steering gear was quite revolutionary and featured a divided track-rod layout. The idea was to try and eliminate some of the 'kickback' associated with the earlier conventional systems. Although somewhat expensive, this system appeared to overcome the problem to a

certain degree and was successful enough to be adopted on all the K series cars as well as the MG racing cars in 1933-34. Basically the steering box operated a transverse draglink which was attached to an idler arm to the left of centre of the beam axle. Two short track rods were also attached to this idler which then attached to the stub axles.

The model range was extended further in early 1933 to add to the previously described confusion by the addition of the L type Magna. This car carried an engine derived from the KB Magnette and became known as the KC type and had coil ignition and twin carburettors. It also had a number of other detail changes including a cheaper dynamo. Despite the ever bewildering range of cars on offer from Abingdon, MG did enjoy very good sales during this period and this no doubt helped to justify probably the most famous Magnette

of all time, the racing K3. The K3 was basically a supercharged K2 with the engine almost standard KB but with the special valves and valve springs and uprated bearings. The chassis was similar to that of the K2 but an addi-

tional cross brace was fitted behind the gearbox. Braking was improved with cast iron liners fitted into the elektron 13" drums, however the rest of the running gear was essentially the same as the Magnettes. The gearbox was a preselector which allowed instantaneous gearchanging saving precious seconds, provided the driver could remember which gear he had pre-selected! Originally the K3 came with a standard two seater body but later on the car could be had with a lightweight boat-tailed competition body. The K3 had many successes in the hands of such famous names as, Earl Howe, Hugh Hamilton, George Eyston and Count Lurani and remained at the top of its class both in racing and record breaking for the best part of two years, becoming one of the most successful racing cars of all time.

The K type engine took on yet another variant late in 1933 when the original bore and stroke were reverted to, thus giving an increased capacity to 1271cc, this engine became known as the KD and was offered throughout the K series touring range. This variant was in general mated to the pre-selector gearbox and the previous problems of 'creeping' were eradicated by using a clutch between the gearbox and engine which disconnected the drive when neutral was engaged. With new carburation the KD engine produced 25% more power than its predecessors which undoubtedly renewed the interest in the Magnettes. This new variant was however very short lived and within six months an improved cylinder head was fitted together with changes to the crankshaft and cylinder block. These were direct developments from the racing K3s and through other improvements in chassis design a completely new model was introduced in March 1934 to be designated the N type Magnette. The beautifully original 1931 K1 Magnette featured belongs to George Ward. A interesting historical point is that the car at one time was in Cecil Kimber's possession for a period during the early thirties. Kimber had a passion for the K types and one of the most publicised early pictures of him shows Kimber behind the wheel of his special Corsica bodied, supercharged K1.

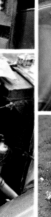

SPECIFICATION
Engine: 6 cylinder in line
Bore/Stroke: 57mm x 71mm
Capacity: 1087cc
Valve operation: Overhead camshaft
Compression ratio: 6.4:1
Induction: Single SU carburettor with Marshall Supercharger.
Transmission: Four speed manual crash box
Brakes: 13″ Drums, cable operated
Suspension: Half elliptic front and rear with sliding trunnions. Beam front axle, live rear axle.
Wheelbase: 9′0″
Track: 4′0″
Steering: Marles, worm and peg type.
Wheels: Rudge Whitworth wire spoked.
Number Built: K1 tourer – 97. K1 saloon – 74. K2 – 20. K3 – 33.

# K3 Magnette

The K3 Magnette must rank in the history books as the most famous and successful of all the record breaking MGs. With only 33 examples produced during 1933 and 1934 this car alone gave an incredible boost to the marque and established MG firmly in the forefront of the world motor racing and record breaking league. Cecil Kimber relied heavily on record breaking and racing successes to promote the marque and increase sales of the everyday cars.

The K series MGs were launched at the London Motor Show in the autumn of 1932 and complimented the already popular Magna range of cars that had appeared the previous year. Great interest was aroused however in the new K series with the main attraction being the racing version the K3. Cecil Kimber was very keen to gain an entry into Class G (1100cc) racing which was previously impossible with the 847 cc Midgets and the 1271cc F type Magnas and whilst he could not justify the production of a model solely for competition, the K3 gave him the chance fulfil this ambition as it could be produced in limited numbers alongside the standard K1 and K2 variants. Although announced at the show there was not a K3 to be seen in the flesh until January of the following year when a prototype K3 emerged from the Abingdon factory.

Initially the K types were available in two chassis lengths with the K1 having a wheelbase of 9' 0" and the K2 being 7' 10" in common with the K3. A track of 4'0" was standard to each model. The MG model range was already quite varied and particularly confusing and now the permutations available on the K series did nothing but add to the confusion. The three models K1,K2 and K3 carried combinations of four different engines. (KA,KB,KD and K3) and three different gearboxes all fitted into five different body variations. it is little wonder that no two cars seemed alike! All the power units carried the 57mm bore of the earlier engines but had a stroke of 71 mm to give a cubic capacity of 1087cc which gave Kimber his much desired entry into Class G for racing and record breaking purposes. To add to the bewildering array of cars described above, early in 1933 the Magna range was enhanced with the addition of the L type that sported an engine derived from the KB Magnette and this was designated the KC type engine and had coil ignition and twin carburettors. Despite the ever increasing selection of MGs and the potential customer spoilt for choice, Abingdon sales soared and there is no doubt that this helped justify Kimbers' development of the most famous MG of all time, the racing K3.

The competitions department at Abingdon produced two K3 prototypes during the winter of 1932, each one carried supercharged 1100cc engines on specially made chassis that had modified C type racing bodies. One of these prototypes was entered on the Monte Carlo Rally and was timed as the quickest car up the Mont des Mules hill climb, easily breaking the previous class record. Car number two accompanied Reg Jackson and a team of drivers to Italy for testing prior to an entry in the gruelling Mille Miglia which was a very tough 1000 mile race on public roads that had to date been dominated by home teams such as Maserati. During an arduous two months test programme several shortcomings were found that were reported back to the engineers at Abingdon who were busy preparing three cars ready for the assault. Earl Howe teamed up with Hugh Hamilton, George Eyston with Count Lurani and the third car carried Henry Birkin and Bernard Rubin. Victory ensued for two cars whilst Birkin had to retire with a broken valve, however Howe and Eyston managed to break all existing class records. finishing first and second in their class, they also collected the team prize. This marvellous performance was achieved at an event that was renowned for being the toughest in the racing world and it set the stage for countless other successes at race venues all over the world. In its class the K3 remained at the top for the best part of two years and was campaigned very successfully by many famous drivers up to the outbreak of war.

Production K3s were based on the standard K2 chassis and this was an open channel frame stiffened with tubular cross members and cruciform centre bracing.The rear axle was underslung the chassis. Suspension was by semi elliptic leaf springs front and rear which were taped and then cord bound. The main spring leaves moved in sliding trunnions at the trailing end. Two Hartford Duplex friction dampers were mounted longitudinally at the front and four were utilised at the rear mounted transversely. Wheels were of the Rudge Whitworth wire spoked racing type and 19" in diameter. Brakes were 13" drum type, operated by via a central cross shaft connected to a fly-off type handbrake lever. The brakes were adjustable via a small hand wheel mounted at the rear of the pre-selector gear lever. The steering gear was quite revolutionary and featured a divided trackrod layout. The idea was to try and eliminate some of the "kick back" associated with the earlier more conventional systems. The gearbox was of the Wilson pre-selector type which allowed instantaneous gearchanging and saved precious seconds when in competition.

The 1933 specification K3s carried a 23.5 gallon slab fuel tank with twin quick release racing type filler caps. Twin electric fuel pumps, one main and one reserve, fed a single SU carburettor mounted above the Power Plus vein type supercharger. In the 1934 cars, modifications implemented included a larger 27.5 gallon fuel tank that was now incorporated into the new pointed boat tail, a hand pump mounted on the dashboard was incorporated into the fuel system to maintain petrol supply by air pressure which dispensed with the need for a battery to run electric pumps. The original specification of the electrical system included a magneto and a dynamo charging twin 6 volt batteries, together with headlamps, torpedo side lamps,

tail lamps, twin horns and a windscreen wiper. All of these circuits were separately switched and fused. In 1934 the cars were further modified and carried special external contacts to couple up to auxiliary starter batteries. Quality dashboard instrumentation was comprehensive with Jaeger equipment that included: Large tachometer, oil pressure gauge, oil and water thermometers, fuel gauge, oil tank gauge, ammeter, supercharger boost and supercharger oil pressure gauges. In standard form the 6 cylinder engine was 1087cc with bore and stroke of 57mm x 71mm. The head was of the cross flow type with a single overhead camshaft driven from the crankshaft via a vertical drive shaft. The shaft also formed part the armature for the vertically mounted dynamo. Special valves and triple springs were used on both inlet and exhaust valves and all bearings had special metalling applied. The Power Plus supercharger was mounted ahead of the radiator and was driven via a splined coupling with universal joints from the crankshaft nose. Power was transferred to the road wheels via the Wilson pre selector gearbox an a three quarter floating rear axle with straight cut bevel gears. The standard exhaust system was a Brooklands competition type with a fixed branch primary manifold feeding to an externally mounted silencer through to a huge fishtail tailpipe. MG devotee Peter Green is the proud owner of the 1933 K3 Magnette featured. MG 3570 has quite a history with some famous pre-war racing drivers having sat behind the wheel. Witney Straight and Dick Seaman are just two worthy of note who had successes with the car during 1933 and 1934.

# K3 MAGNETTE

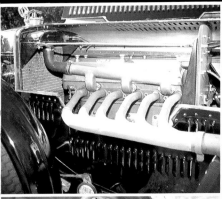

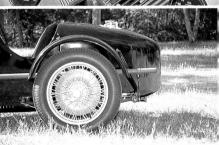

MG 3570

570

## SPECIFICATION
Engine: 6 cylinder in line.
Bore/Stroke: 57mm x 71mm.
Capacity: 1087cc.
Valve operation: Overhead camshaft via vertical shaft.
Carburation: Single SU through supercharger.
Power output: Between 100 and 120 bhp dependent on type of supercharger and state of tune.
Transmission: Wilson pre-selector four speed epicyclic gearbox.
Brakes: 12" cable operated vented ribbed drum all round.
Chassis: Twin side members with cross bracing.
Suspension: Half elliptic front and rear with sliding trunnions.
Beam axle front, live rear axle.
Wheelbase: 7' 10 3/16" Track: 4'0" front and rear. Wheels: Centre-lock Rudge Whitworth wire spoke.
Number built 1933-1934 inc prototypes: 33
Cost new chassis only: £675.

# KN Magnette pillarless saloon

A surprise was in store for MG enthusiasts at the 1932 Motor Show with the last minute launch of a new series of 6 cylinder cars designated Magnette. The already popular Magna

range of MGs or "Light Sixes" as they were often referred to, continued in production alongside the smaller engined overhead cam J types. The six cylinder cars did not generate quite the same following as the four cylinder high revving stablemates, nonetheless they fulfilled a market need aimed at those enthusiasts who wanted a bit more refinement and could afford to pay for it. The six cylinder cars were produced in relatively small numbers compared to the Midgets of the era, mainly due to the cost and performance penalties, but the decision was taken to follow the example set by some of the European manufacturers who had found a successful formula in small capacity, low geared power units that could easily move heavyweight chassis.

The trend towards the six cylinder cars can be appreciated when you consider that most of the four cylinder cars that were available in the early 1930's had solidly mounted engines and "crash" gearboxes. The small six cylinder cars ran a lot more smoothly with minimal vibration and had plenty of torque which negated the endless gear changes normally necessary in the four cylinder cars. The price penalty manifested itself in the end cost of the six cylinder cars and also the horsepower tax rating which meant that a six cylinder engine of 1100 cc to 1300 cc paid as much tax as a 1500 cc four cylinder car. The performance penalty was in the form of very small bore diameters with long stroke to reduce the engine capacity (in keeping with the horsepower tax formula) and whilst the acceleration was far from exhilarat-

ing, high speed cruising was a pleasure. The origins of the MG 'light six' cars stemmed from the Wolseley Hornet, first produced in 1930 and Cecil Kimber realised that with the

impending demise of the large six cylinder 18/80's that appealed to the wealthier MG fraternity, he had to find a mid-range replacement. The Wolseley Hornet, coming from the same family, was an ideal candidate to "borrow" ideas and parts from. The delightfully smooth 12 hp engine was to be the basis to power Kimber's new F type Magna launched in September 1931. Abingdon tried to pretend that this engine was a brand new design with the engineers cleverly tacking two extra cylinders on and camouflaging the cylinder block with sheet steel to disguise its Wolseley origins. The F type was very well received and priced at £250 for the open two seater, was good value compared to the 18/80 MkII at £625. It sold steadily despite its disappointing performance but the hankering for better 6 cylinder performance soon brought Kimber to introduce a new range of cars with a view to extending Abingdon's participation in Class G (1100cc) motor sport. Kimber could not justify the production of a model just for competition but the K series Magnettes allowed him to conceal an out and out racing model amongst the more sedate saloons and open topped touring cars in the range.

Named Magnette, the range fell midway between the 847 cc Midgets and the 1271 cc Magnas and although the Magnettes cost over £100 more than their Magna counterparts, Abingdon was keen to point out in the sales literature that the engine was of completely new design and was sturdy enough to take a supercharger without modification, which empha-

sised the racing intentions. The brochure described the engine thus; "The overhead camshaft engine of this series is entirely new, consequently there is a very big margin of safety as produced in unsupercharged form". The new K Magnette chassis was available in two different wheelbase lengths, one of 9' 0" exactly and the other of 7' 10.1875". The longer chassis carried the open top 4 seater tourer or the unusual closed 4 door saloon which had no central door pillar and became known as the KN "pillarless" saloon. This shapely and well proportioned MG was favourably received by the motoring press and performed reasonably well for a heavy sports saloon. Priced at £445 it was not considered cheap, nonetheless the car was well appointed and very comfortable. On the shorter chassis there were options of a two seater sports and two versions of the K3 racing car, one supercharged and one unsupercharged. The K series cars had several different versions of the 1086 cc engine unit fitted and they were designated KA, KB, KD and K3. There were also three different types of gearbox fitted, add this to the five alternative body styles together with the small build quantities and you will realise that no two vehicles ever seemed to be identical.

The new six cylinder Magnette engine was loosely based on the Wolseley Hornet design with the stroke reduced from 83 mm to 71 mm to give an engine capacity of 1087cc. Other refinements included large diameter 13" brakes (cable operated) and an improved steering system that incorporated a divided track rod to try and eliminate the common problem of "steering wheel kick back" normally encountered on conventional beam axle systems. The cylinder head was of cross-flow design and ignition was by magneto. A preselector gearbox was employed which at the time were much in vogue and whilst other manufacturers normally mounted the selector lever on the steering column, MG placed a very neat and stubby selector lever on the top of the gearbox itself ensuring rapid selection. The KA engine, as installed exclusively in the Saloon, had a special "slower" camshaft to allow the fitment of the ENV preselector gearbox as the engine tickover speed needed to be kept below 500 rpm to avoid the car creeping unless checked by the brakes. The KB engine had standard valve timing with the four speed gearbox being driven through a twin plate dry clutch and was installed in KI two and four seaters. The KC engine, just to throw in some confusion, had coil ignition and was not fitted to any K type, instead was used to power a new F type replacement, designated the L type Magna that appeared in 1933. The K3 engine was used both in supercharged and unsupercharged form in the K3 racing cars. The KD engine was available in late 1933 and reverted back to the original bore and stroke which increased the capacity to 1271cc. This power unit was then offered to the whole range of K types and was normally combined with the preselector gearbox. The problems of "creeping" associated with the standard valve timing were overcome with the by utilising a clutch between the gearbox and engine that disconnected the drive once neutral was selected. A 25% increase in power was gained by the new KD engine which transformed the cars performance considerably. The 1934 KN Saloon featured belongs to Peter Moores.

SPECIFICATION

Engine: 6 Cylinder in line.

Capacity: KA, KB: 1086cc. KD: 1271cc.
K3: 1087cc

Bore: 57mm.

Stroke: KA, KB, K3: 71mm. KD: 83mm.

Power Output:
KA: 39bhp @ 5,500rpm
KB: 41bhp @ 5,500rpm
KD: 48bhp @ 5,500rpm
K3: approx 120bhp @ 6,500rpm.

Valve operation: Single overhead camshaft driven through vertical dynamo.

Carburation: KA, KD: 3xSU, OM.
KD: 2xSU HV2
K3: SU HV8.

Gearbox: KA, KD: ENV preselector.
KB: 4 speed Manual.

Brakes: 13" drum, cable operated.

Chassis: Steel channel with tubular cross members.

Suspension: Half elliptic front & rear with sliding trunnions.

Wheelbase: K1: 9'0". K2: 7'10.1875"

Track: 4'0".

Steering: Marles worm and peg type.

Numbers produced:
K1 Tourer: 97. K1 Saloon: 74. K2: 20.
Chassis only: 35. K3: 33.

# K3 Magnette Racer

The K' series MGs were introduced in 1932 at the London Motor Show, they were to compliment the already successful Magna range of cars and were designated 'K' type in logical

sequence following on from the very popular 'J' types. The K1 and K2 models utilised the now familiar and well established conventional MG chassis layout. These new models were to form the basis for an important new racing model and it was with this solely in mind that Cecil Kimber took the decision to produce the K1 and K2, as he was unable to justify the production of a racing model on its own at the time. Kimber was keen to get an entry into Class G (1100cc) racing, and as this class fell midway between the 847cc Midgets and 1271 cc Magnas, it was decided to produce a special racing model the K3. Although this was announced at the 1932 Motor Show, at the same time as the K1 and K2, it was not until January 1933 that a prototype emerged from the factory that would give Kimber chance to compete in Class G.

The MG model range was particularly confusing at this time with the K' series having three different chassis, four different engines, three different gearboxes and five body variations. With such small quantities of each one being produced, no two cars seemed alike! To add to this confusion early on in 1933, the Magna range was updated with the introduction of the 'L' type in which was placed an engine derived from the KB Magnette power unit. This became known as the K3 type with coil ignition and twin carburettors, despite this ever increasing and confusing range of cars, Abingdon did achieve very good sales during this period, and this no doubt helped Kimber to justify the introduction of probably the most famous Magnette of all time, the racing K3.

During the Winter of 1932/33 two K3 prototypes were produced in the Racing Department at the Abingdon factory. Both utilised supercharged 1100cc engines on specially made chassis upon which were mounted modified 'C' type racing bodies. One of the cars was entered in the Monte Carlo Rally and it proved to be the fastest car on the Mont Des Mules hill climb section and it broke the class record easily. The other car went with a team of drivers led by Reg Jackson to Italy to tackle the gruelling Mille Miglia. This 1000 mile road race on public roads had always been dominated by such home teams as Maserati. The prototype was put through its paces around sections of the Mille Miglia course on a reconnaissance mission prior to the event. The idea behind this was to thoroughly test the car and

show up any weaknesses that were not immediately apparent. This proved a worthwhile exercise and as a result the pre-selector gearbox was revised because the gearing was too low and it also consumed too much oil. Road wheels and hubs were also redesigned as were the brake drums which failed under the arduous two months testing programme. Meanwhile back in Abingdon, three team cars were prepared and were shipped to Genoa in early March 1933 in readiness to tackle Mille Miglia. The three cars were to be driven by Earl Howe and Hugh Hamilton, George Eyston and Count Lurani with a third car manned by Henry Birkin and Bernard Rubin. Birkin's K3 had to retire with a broken valve, but the remaining two K3s proceeded to break all existing class records, finishing first and second in their Class and they also came away with the coveted team prize. The Mille Miglia was renowned for being the toughest racing event in the World and the MG victory at this event set the stage for countless other successes at race venues all over the World. In its Class the K3 remained at the top for the best part of two years, and became one of the most successful racing cars of all time.

The production K3s were based on the standard K2 chassis and this was an open-channel frame stiffened with tubular cross-members and cruciform centre bracing, the axle was underslung beneath the rear axle. Remote chassis lubrication was provided by grouped oil nipples mounted on a plate on the offside bulk head. Suspension was by semi-elliptic leaf springs front and rear which were taped and then cord bound. The main spring leaves moved in sliding trunnions at the trailing end. Two Hartford Duplex friction dampers were mounted longitudinally at the front and four were utilised at the rear mounted transversely. Wheels were of the Rudge Whitworth wired spoked racing type and 19" in diameter. Brakes were 13" drum type cable operated via a central cross-shaft connected to a fly-off type handbrake lever. The brakes were adjustable from the cockpit via a small hand wheel mounted on the back of the gearbox below the preselector lever. The steering was effected by means of a cam type box and transverse drag link to an axle mounted slave arm that controlled the wheels through a divided track rod. The 1933 specification cars originally carried a 23.5 gallon slab type fuel tank, with a three gallon reserve and twin quick release racing filler caps. Twin electric fuel pumps one main and one reserve fed into a single SU carburettor mounted above the power plus vein type supercharger. In 1934 the cars were modified and a larger 27.5 gallon fuel tank was fitted that was formed into a pointed tail, a hand pump was incorporated in the fuel system to

maintain the fuel supply by air pressure which dispensed with a need for a battery. The original specification electrical system included a magneto, a dynamo charging twin 6 volt batteries, headlamps, torpedo sidelamps, tail lamps, twin horns, and a windscreen wiper. All of these circuits were separately switched and fused. In 1934 the cars were further modified and carried special external contacts to couple up to auxiliary starter batteries. Dashboard instrumentation was comprehensive with quality Jaeger equipment to include Tachometer, Oil Pressure Gauge, Oil and Water Thermometers, Fuel Gauge, Oil Tank Gauge, Ammeter, Supercharger Boost Gauge, and Supercharger Oil Pressure Gauge.

In the standard production K3 cars the six cylinder overhead camshaft engine had a bore and stroke of 57mm x 71mm with a displacement of 1086cc. The four main bearing crankshaft carried steel connecting rods with aluminium pistons. Engine lubrication was effected by a wet sump system utilising a gear driven pump and large triangular shaped finned sump which greatly assisted with oil cooling. A reserve oil feed tank was mounted on the scuttle. The standard cylinder head was of the cross flow type with a single overhead camshaft driven by a vertical shaft directly from the crankshaft. This shaft also formed the armature for the vertically mounted dynamo. Special valves and triple springs were used on both inlet and exhaust and bearings all had special metalling applied. The power plus vein type supercharger was mounted ahead of the radiator and was driven via a splined coupling shaft with universal joints directly from the crankshaft nose. A Wilson pre-selector gearbox with centrally mounted selector lever transferred the power to the road wheels via a 3/4 floating rear axle with straight cut bevel final drive. The standard exhaust system was a Brooklands competition type with a fixed branch primary manifold feeding to an externally mounted silencer which then lead to a huge fishtail tail pipe. A thermosyphon cooling system was employed with an engine driven water pump.

The featured car is very much a one-off K3 Racer and it originally started life from the Abingdon Works as a two seater car in 1933. It was then converted in 1934 to an offset single seater race car by Ron Horton. The car then changed hands in 1935 and over the following four years was progressively and extensively modified by the well known driver of the era Reg Parnell. Following a bad accident in practice for an event, the front end of the car was extensively damaged and when rebuilt was fitted with Lancia independent front suspension and larger 14" drum brakes. The car was raced with considerable success at Brooklands and Donington race circuits prior to the war. Throughout the 1950s the car was to see one or two appearances at different race circuits before being finally laid up in 1964. It was restored in 1985 by Peter Gregory the six cylinder MG specialist of Goring-on-Thames.

# K3 Racer

SPECIFICATION

The following data is for a Standard K3:

Engine: 6 cylinder in line

Bore/Stroke: 57mm x 71mm

Capacity: 1087cc

Valve Operation: Overhead camshaft.

Compression ratio: 5.4:1 to 6.6:1 according to tune.

Induction: Single SU carburettor with Powerplus or Marshall Supercharger.

Power Output: 105 to 125bhp according to state of tune.

Transmission: Wilson pre-selector four speed gearbox without clutch.

Brakes: 13″ drum, cable operated, (twin lever 1934).

Suspension: Half elliptic front and rear with sliding trunnions.

Beam axle front, live rear axle.

Chassis: Twin side members with cross members.

Wheelbase: 7′10³/₁₆″

Track: 4′0″ front and rear.

Wheels: Centre lock wire spoke.

Weight: 18¼ cwts.

Performance: Max speed: 110mph.

Acceleration: 0-75mph in 14.6 secs. Fuel consumption: approx 15 mpg.

Number built including prototypes and EX135: 33

Price new £675 for chassis only or £795 complete.

**Special Bodied K3 Racer**

Specification as above with the following modifications:

Brakes: Girling 14″ drums hydraulically operated.

Suspension: Front; Lancia independent with telescopic dampers.

Induction: Single SU carburettor with special Burke Supercharger.

Performance figures not available.

# L1 Magna Continental Coupé

Most MGs are commonly thought of as 4 cylinder cars, the modern exceptions are of course the MGC and MGB GT V8, however in earlier times there was a tradition of 6 cylinder MGs starting with the 18/80 range that was introduced in 1928. The cars that really set the foundation of this tradition were the MG Magnas and Magnettes that were produced between 1932 and 1936, the most popular being the F type Magna with a production run of 1250 cars. There was a definite gap in the MG range in the early thirties and Cecil Kimber realised that they had to produce something midway between the very successful 8 horsepower Midgets and at the other end of the scale the 18/80 range. In 1930 the Wolseley Hornet was introduced, powered by a delightfully smooth 12 horsepower engine, however the rest of the car was totally uninspiring and although Kimber no doubt thought that a 12 horsepower Midget was a good idea, nothing materialised due to all effort being concentrated on the double Twelve M Type Midget and the C type Montlhéry Midget.

The first 12 horsepower Magna was introduced in September 1931 and was known as 'the light six'. This car was to be the MG Car Company's venture into the smoother running six cylinder sports car market and was basically a C type that was stretched by 10" in length and powered by an M type engine that had two extra cylinders added. The hefty power unit was taken straight from the Wolseley Hornet but was camouflaged by MG engineers externally. Twin carburettors helped produced a modest 37 bhp and performance was less than startling and the car sold well if only that it looked the part. The six cylinder cars were however to be produced in relatively small numbers compared to the Midgets of the era as they did not generate quite the same affection performance wise. Although smooth, they did not give quite the exhilaration of the smaller MGs. The appeal for the six cylinder cars was nonetheless understandable when you consider that most of the 1930's cars had solidly mounted engines and non-synchromesh gearboxes and when directly compared with their four cylinder counterparts, the 'light sixes' ran far smoother with less vibration.

The K types followed in 1932 and will be long remembered for their numerous racing successes. The MG range of models was already quite varied when at the Motor Show of that year the K series was launched. Following on in logical sequence from the very popular J types, the K1 and K2 utilised the now familiar and well established conventional MG chassis layout. A 1096cc power unit was employed and was an improved version of that used in the Magna with a stronger crankshaft and a cross-flow cylinder head. There were several versions offered and each one was a little different from the other with chassis and engine variations. There was also a racing version on offer designated the K3. To add to the confusion there were also four different body options; four seat saloon, four seat tourer, four seat open and two seat open. It goes without saying that with this confusing array of options available, the cars were only produced in relatively small numbers. At this time Abingdon were not only producing a bewildering assortment of competition cars but the company's production cars were to become even more varied with the introduction of the L type Magnas in March 1933.

The new improved Magna shared the shorter stroke six cylinder engine used in the K Magnette. The engine known as the KC type

was in fact a KB unit with coil ignition and twin carburettors. The shorter stroke of 57mm x 71mm was identical to the racing Midgets of the time and with a capacity of 1086cc it put the new car neatly in the 1100cc class. An important innovation on this engine was the new cross flow cylinder head with six ports on each side, this boosted power to 41 bhp at 5500 rpm. The KB clutch and 4 speed gearbox of Wolseley origins were employed which were essentially the same as those fitted to the J type Midgets. The L types were genuine 75 mph motor cars and were considered better than their predecessors. They did however retain the characteristic sloping radiator that was a feature of the previous Magnas and they were fitted with flowing swept wings of similar design to the then current J type Midgets. The L types utilised a long wheelbase version of the K series chassis but with a track of 3' 6" instead of the K series 4' 0" track. The L1 was a four seater car with an option of an open or closed body and the L2 was an open two seater tourer, similar in appearance to other MGs of the period adopting same body styles of earlier Magnas and Magnettes. There was an exception however and this was the model featured; the L1 Continental Coupé. Cecil Kimber could not resist the temptation to experiment with saloon based models and this

particular offering from Abingdon became affectionately known as 'Kimbers Folly'. Unfortunately the car did not sell particularly well and it is reported by Mike Allison in "Magic of MG" that one hundred were made and they took as many weeks to sell!

The Continental Coupé was available in bright two-tone colour schemes, generally canary yellow and black and its coachbuilt body was to the highest standard. Fairly innovative was the rear end styling which on first inspection gives the impression of a large boot for luggage stowage. This could not be further from the truth for inside there is only just room for the petrol tank at the back of the compartment with the spare wheel shoehorned in for good measure. Atop the boot was an elaborate fairing which incorporated an illuminated number plate, brake and stop lights and originally an early form of direction indicator (these have been replaced on the featured car for safety reasons). The interior was well appointed if not a little cramped and could really only accommodate two adults in comfort, but an occasional rear seat was provided that would normally be occupied by accompanying luggage. A feature of the car was the delightful sliding glass sunroof which could be adjusted to give controlled ventilation and at the same time allow light into the cockpit making it less claustrophobic.

# L1 Continental Coupe

SPECIFICATION

Engine: 6 cylinder in line.
Capacity: 1086cc.
Bore and Stroke: 57mm x 71mm.
Valve Gear: Overhead camshaft driven through vertical dynamo.
Carburation: Twin semi-downdraught SU's.
Power output: 41 bhp at 5,500 rpm.
Gearbox: 4 speed non-synchromesh 'crash' gearbox.
Brakes: Bowden cable operated 12'' drums.
Clutch: Dry plate.
Suspension: Half elliptic front and rear with sliding trunnions.
Wheels: Centre lock wire spoke.
Wheelbase: 7' 10 3/16''.
Track: 3' 6'' front and rear.
Max Speed: 75 mph.
Fuel consumption: approx 23 mpg.
Weight: 16 cwts.
Number built: 100 Continental Coupe; 486 (total of all variant body styles).

In the early thirties there was a definite gap in the MG range with the 8 horsepower Midgets selling well and at the other end of the scale the 18/80 range which appealed to the more

wealthy MG fraternity. With the demise of the old side valve cars. Cecil Kimber had to produce something midway between the Midgets and the 18/80s. The Wolseley Hornet was introduced in 1930 and was powered by a delightfully smooth 12 horsepower engine. The rest of the car was totally uninspiring and did not seem a good basis for a sports model, merely being a stretched Morris Minor! There is no doubt that Kimber had considered a 12 horsepower Midget but the idea never materialised simply because all efforts were concentrated on the Double Twelve M type Midget and the C type Montlhéry Midget.

It was not until September 1931 that the first 12 horsepower Magna was introduced, known as a 'light six'. This car was to be the MG Car Company's venture into the smoother running six cylinder sports car market. The six cylinder cars were however to be produced in relatively small numbers compared to the Midgets of the era as they did not generate quite the same affection. Performance wise, although smooth, they did not give quite the exhilaration of the smaller MGs. The appeal for the six cylinder cars was nonetheless understandable when you consider that most of the 1930s cars had solidly mounted engines and non synchromesh gearboxes and when directly compared with their four cylinder counterparts, the 'light sixes' ran far smoother with far less vibration. The first and the most popular of the Magnas was the F type which had a production run of 1250 cars. The car was basically a C type that was stretched by 10" in length and it was powered by an M type engine that had two extra cylinders 'tacked' on. The hefty power unit was derived straight from the Wolseley Hornet but was cunningly camouflaged externally by MG engineers. Twin carburettors helped to produce a modest 37 bhp and performance was adequate, certainly not startling, however the car sold well if only because it looked the part. There were two body styles available, a four seat tourer and a close coupled salonette. 1250 cars were produced in just over 12 months which was a good figure by MG standards. An improved model was introduced at the 1932 Motor Show with better, larger brakes. In total 129 of these were produced either in two seater form, known as the F2 or in four seater guise designated the F3. Following closely in 1932 were the K type

Magnettes which will be remembered for their racing successes. The MG model range was already quite varied when at the Motor Show of that year the K series MGs were launched. The cars followed on in logical sequence from the very popular J types and the K1 and K2 utilised the now familiar and well established conventional MG chassis layout. A 1086cc power unit was employed and was an improved version of that used in the Magna with a stronger crankshaft and a cross-flow cylinder head. There were several versions offered and each one a little different from the other with chassis and engine variations. There was also a racing version designated K3. To add to the confusion there were also four different body options; four seat saloon, four seat tourer, four seat open and two seat open. Needless to say with this confusing array of options available, the cars were only produced in relatively small quantities. At this time Abingdon were not only producing a bewildering array of competition cars but the company's production cars were to become even more varied with the introduction of the L type Magnas in March 1933.

The new improved Magna shared the shorter stroke six cylinder engine used in the K type Magnette. The engine known as the KC type was in fact a KB unit with coil ignition and twin carburettors. The shorter stroke of 57mm x 71mm was identical to the racing Midgets of the era and with a capacity of 1086cc it put the new car neatly in the 1100cc class. An important innovation on this engine was the new cross flow cylinder head with six ports on each side, this boosted the power to 41 bhp at 5500rpm. The KB clutch and 4 speed gearbox of Wolseley origins were employed which were essentially

the same as those fitted to the J type Midgets. The L types were genuine 75mph motor cars and were considered better than their predecessors. They did however retain the characteristic sloping radiator that was a feature of previous Magnas and they were fitted with flowing swept wings of similar design to the current J type Midgets. The L types utilised a long wheelbase version of the K series chassis but with a track of 3' 6" instead of the K series 4' 0" track. The L1 was a four seater car with an option of an open or closed body and the L2 was an open two seater tourer, similar in appearance to other MGs of the period adopting same body styles as earlier Magnas and Magnettes, with the exception of the Continental Coupé which was introduced at the 1933 Motor Show. The Continental proved rather unpopular at the time of production and very few were made, thus making it an extremely rare MG.

The body types that were available were somewhat confusing at first glance. The L type Magna looked like a large J2 or F2 with K2 type swept wings and this amazing Abingdon jigsaw puzzle did help sales but ultimately reduced overall profits due to the non-commonality of parts. This juggling of parts to produce supposedly new models was typical of many of the car manufacturers of the era, but it led to production and servicing problems due to each individual model requiring greater attention at each of the different stages. Whenever a new innovation was found to be assisting in the sales of a particular model this would where possible be transferred to other models in the range to boost sales of that model and this is why hardly any two Magnas or Magnettes are exactly alike. The L series cars were considerably more expensive than the earlier Magnas and upon introduction were priced at £285 for the two seater L2, £299 for the four seater L1 and £334 for the Salonette.

# L1 MAGNA

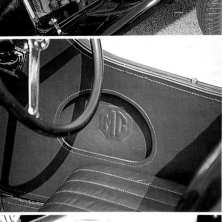

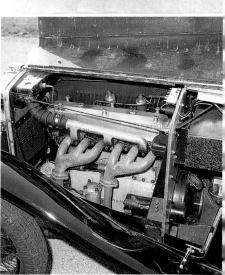

## SPECIFICATION

Engine: 6 cylinder in line
Capacity: 1086cc
Bore and Stroke: 57mm x 71mm
Valve Gear: Overhead camshaft driven through vertical dynamo.
Carburation: Twin semi-downdraught SUs
Power output: 41bhp @ 5,500 rpm
Gearbox: 4 speed non-synchromesh 'crash' gearbox
Brakes: Bowden cable operated 12″ drums.
Clutch: Dry plate.
Suspension: Half elliptic front and rear with sliding trunnions
Wheels: Centre lock wire spoke.
Wheelbase: 7′ 10³/₁₆″
Track: 3′ 6′ front and rear.
Max speed: 75mph
Fuel consumption: approx 23mpg
Weight: 16cwts
Price new in 1933: £299
Number built: 486 (total of all variant body styles)

# L2 Magna

MGs are most commonly thought of as being four cylinder cars apart from one or two exceptions such as the MGC and the MGB GT V8. In earlier years there was a tradition of six cylinder engined cars and the first of which was the 18/80 which was introduced in 1928. The foundation of this tradition rests with the MG Magnas and Magnettes that were produced between 1931 and 1936, the most popular of

which was the first Magna which was the F type with a production run of 1250 cars. This car was basically a C type that was stretched by 10 inches in length and powered by an M type engine with two extra cylinders added on. The hefty power unit was taken straight from the Wolseley Hornet but was camouflaged externally by MG engineers. Twin carburettors helped produce a modest 37 bhp and performance was less than startling, but the car sold well if only for its good looks.

Following closely in 1932 were the K type Magnettes which will be remembered for their racing successes. The MG model range was already quite varied but at the 1932 Motor Show several new models were introduced designated K1 and K2 with different body options. These vehicles used the already established chassis layout but with two different wheelbases of 9' and 7' 10 '' respectively. A 1087 cc engine unit was employed and was an improved version of that used in the Magna but with a stronger crankshaft and a crossflow head. The Magnettes were usually fitted with a non-synchromesh gearbox which is more commonly known as a 'crash' box. Timing gear changes to coincide with engine could produce smooth gearchanges but there was an option of a pre-selector transmission. This worked with the driver selecting a gear by moving a lever and then when needed he would depress the clutch and the gear selection was made effortlessly with both hands still on the steering wheel.

The several versions that were offered were each a little different from the other with chassis and engine variations. There was also a racing version offered, designated K3. To add to the confusion there were also four different body options: Four seat saloon, four seat tourer, four seat open and two seat open. Needless to say with all this bewildering array of options the cars were only produced in relatively small quantities with approximately 71 K1s, 15 K2s and 33 K3s (which includes EX135 the K3 based record car) being built. At this time Cecil Kimber's team were not only producing a bewildering array of competition cars but the company's production cars were becoming even more varied with the launch of the L type Magnas in March 1933.

The L series of cars had an improved K series engine fitted and utilised the long wheelbase K series chassis but with the earlier 3' 6" track instead of the K series 4' 0". The L1 was designated a 4 seater with open or closed body option and the L2 was an open two seat tourer and was very similar in appearance to other

MGs of the period, adopting the same body styles as the earlier Magnas and Magnettes, with the exception of the Continental Coupé which was introduced at the 1933 Motor Show. The Continental proved unpopular at the time of production and very few were made, thus making it an extremely rare car. The body types were confusing because at first glance the L type Magna looked like a large J2 or F2 with K2 type swept wings and this amazing Abingdon jigsaw puzzle did help sales somewhat but reduced overall profits. This juggling of parts to produce new models was typical of many manufacturers of the era but led to production and servicing problems as each model needed individual attention at all the different stages. Whenever a new innovation was found to be assisting in the sales of a particular model this would wherever possible be transferred to other models in the range to boost sales of that model and this is why hardly any two Magnas or Magnettes are exactly alike.

The engine unit for the L type Magna was

known as the KC and was derived from the KB Magnette engine with the shorter stroke of 57mm x 71mm which was identical to the racing Midgets of the era. With a displacement of 1087 cc this put the new Magna engine neatly into the 1100 cc class. An important innovation on the new engine was a new cross-flow cylinder head with six ports on each side. This boosted power to 41 bhp at 5500 rpm with twin carburettors and coil ignition instead of a magneto. The KB clutch and 4 speed gearbox of Wolseley origins were employed which were essentially the same as fitted to the J type Midgets. The L series cars were considerably more expensive than the earlier Magnas and upon introduction were priced at £285 for the two seater, £299 for the four seater and £334 for the Salonette. They were genuine 75mph cars and were considerably better than their predecessors with the characteristic sloping radiator that was a feature of previous Magnas.

# L2 Magna

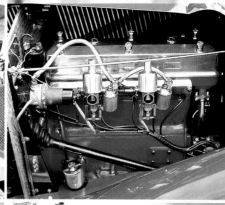
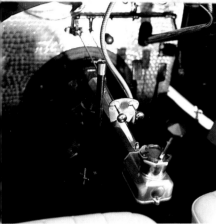

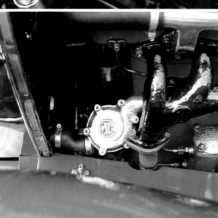

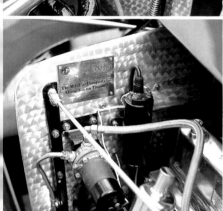
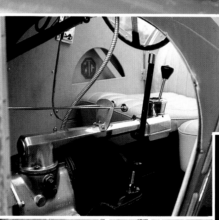

**Specification:**
Engine: 6 cylinder in line
Capacity: 1086cc
Bore and Stroke: 57mm x 71mm
Valve Gear: Overhead Camshaft driven through vertical dynamo
Carburation: Twin semi downdraught SUs
Power output: 41 bhp @ 5500 rpm
Gearbox: 4 speed non-synchromesh 'crash' gearbox
Brakes: Bowden cable operated 12″ drums
Clutch: Dry clutch
Suspension: half elliptic front and rear with sliding trunnions
Wheels: Centre-lock wire spoke
Wheelbase: 7′ 10 3/16″
Track: 3′6″ front and rear
Max speed: 75 mph
Fuel consumption: approx 23 mpg
Weight: 16 cwts
Price in 1933: £285 plus tax of £12
Number built: 90

# L1 Carlton Magna

Six cylinder engines were the vogue in the decade 1925 to 1935 and the reasons for this were mainly due to the unrefined running of the then current four cylinder units. This harshness was further emphasised by the utilisation of solid engine mountings locating the power unit to chassis. It was also a fact that gear changing on the four cylinder cars was a nightmare with heavy clutch operation combined with non-synchronised gears. Weighty flywheels were also adopted to try and smooth things out which in the end tended to highlight the problem rather than alleviate it. The European manufacturers had led the way with the smoother running six cylinder engines having discovered that relatively large bodied cars could be successfully propelled with small capacity low geared engines. MG had already adopted a six cylinder engine in their 18/80 model launched in 1928 but it was not until 1931 that Abingdon announced a light six in the form of the F type Magna. This 12 horsepower car was to be the MG Car Company's venture into the six cylinder sports car market and was to prove the most popular of the Magnas and Magnettes produced over the period 1931 to 1936.

Cecil Kimber had realised with the demise of the old side valve cars that there was a definite gap in the MG model range and that a sports car midway between the very successful 8 horsepower Midgets and at the top end the large 18/80 range, needed to be produced. In 1930 the Wolseley Hornet was introduced with a beautifully smooth 12 horsepower engine, but the rest of the car remained totally uninspiring. There is no doubt that Cecil Kimber considered the possibilities of a 12 horsepower Midget, but this never materialised due to all efforts being concentrated on the Double Twelve M type Midget and the racing C Type Montlhéry Midget. With a production run of 1250 cars the F type was basically a C type that was stretched by 10 feet in length and powered by an M type engine with two extra cylinders 'tacked on'. The hefty power unit was taken straight from the aforementioned Wolseley Hornet but camouflaged by MG engineers externally. Twin carburettors helped produce a modest 37 bhp and performance was less than startling but the car sold well if only because of its good looks. Following on closely in 1932 were the K types which will be long remembered for their numerous racing successes. Launched at the Motor Show of that year, the K1 and K2 utilised the now familiar

and well tried conventional MG chassis layout. A 1096cc power unit was employed which was a stronger version of that used in the Magna, utilising a sturdier crankshaft and a cross flow cylinder head. There were several K types offered and each one was slightly different from the other with chassis and engine variations. There was also a racing version designated K3. To confuse matters further there were also four different types of body option offered and this serves to illustrate why these cars were only produced in relatively small numbers. At this time Cecil Kimber's team were not only producing a confusing array of competition cars but the company's production cars were to become even more varied with

the introduction of the L Type Magnas in March 1933.

This new car carried the KC type engine and was the direct replacement for the F type Magna. With a shorter stroke than the F type it sported twin carburettors and coil ignition and with a capacity of 1086 cc put the new MG neatly into the 1100 cc class. An important innovation on the new engine was the crossflow cylinder head with six ports on each side and this boosted power to 41 bhp at 5.500 rpm. The KB clutch and 4 speed gearbox of Wolseley origins were employed and were essentially the same as those fitted to the J type Midgets. The L1 was designated a four seater in open tourer or closed body options. The L2 was strictly a two seater sports car and was very similar in appearance to other MGs of the period, adopting same body styles as other earlier Magnas or Magnettes, with the exception of the Continental Coupé which was introduced at the 1933 Motor Show. The Continental proved unpopular at the time of production and very few were made thus making it an extremely rare car. The body types were confusing. because at first glance, the L type Magna looked like a large J2 or F2 with K2 type swept wings and although this amazing Abingdon jigsaw puzzle boosted sales somewhat it ultimately reduced profitability. This juggling of parts to produce new models was typical of many of the manufacturers of the era but led to production and servicing problems as each model needed individual attention through all the different production stages. Whenever a new innovation was found to be assisting in the sales of a particular model this would then be transferred to other models in the range to boost sales and this is the reason why no two models of Magnas or Magnettes are exactly alike.

The L types were genuine 75 mph motor cars and were considered better cars than their predecessors. They retained the characteristic sloping radiator that was a feature of previous Magnas and they were fitted with flowing swept wings similar to the then current J type Midgets. The L types utilised a long wheelbase version of the K series chassis but with a track of 3' 6" instead of the K type 4' 0" track. The L series were considerably more expensive than the earlier Magnas and upon introduction were priced at £285 for the two seater L2 and £299 for the four seater L1. The Salonette version of which only 97 were made was priced at £334. Records indicate that 31 chassis only were produced by Abingdon and it is possible that these were forwarded on to specialist coach builders and it is likely that a fair number of these were acquired by University Motors for conversion on their behalf by the Carlton Carriage Company to a coachbuilt drophead coupe. This delightful conversion was economically priced at £385 and although it is not clear precisely how many Carlton bodied L1 Magnas were produced, the beautiful example featured is believed to be the only surviving

example. Bearing chassis number L0616 the Magna was first registered in 1934 and unfortunately little is known about the cars early history. BPC 479 is presently owned by Anthony Littlejohn.

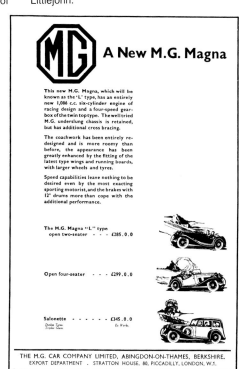

# L1 CARLTON MAGNA

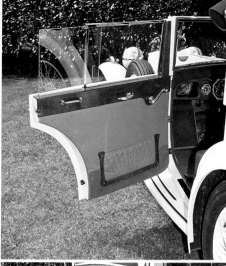

## SPECIFICATION

Engine: 6 Cylinder in line
Capacity: 1086 cc
Bore & Stroke: 57mm x 71 mm
Valve Gear: Overhead camshaft driven through vertical dynamo
Carburation: Twin semi-downdraft SU HV2
Power output: 41 bhp at 5,500 rpm
Gearbox: 4 speed non-synchromesh 'crash' gearbox
Brakes: Bowden cable operated 12" drums
Steering: Marles box, worm and peg
Clutch: Twin dry plate
Suspension: Half elliptic front and rear with sliding trunnions
Wheels: Centre lock Rudge wire spoke
Wheelbase: 7' 10 3/16"
Track: 3' 6" front and rear
Max speed: 75 mph
Fuel consumption: approx 23 mpg
Number built: unknown

# NA Magnette Airline Coupé

The name Magnette was first used on an MG by Cecil Kimber in 1932 when the K series of cars were announced. The designation Magna preceded the Magnette range, first appearing on the F type in 1931. The F type in particular was derived from the C and D type Midgets that were launched in the same year. It is from the Midget, Magna and Magnette range of MGs that the terminology, Triple M cars originated. The advent of the Magnette name on the K series cars heralded the arrival of the 'Light Sixes' as they became known. The heavy 18/80s were nearing the end of their useful production life, although they still appealed to the more wealthy MG fraternity. 6 cylinder engines were very popular in the decade 1925-1935, simply because the 4 cylinder engines of the period were very harsh running units. This harshness became accentuated by the use of solid engine mounts direct onto the chassis. This coupled with non-synchromesh gearboxes, heavy clutches and weighty flywheels all added up to a less than satisfactory package. Low engine speed emphasised the unevenness of the 4 cylinder engines and constant gearchanging made driving a bit of a chore. Hence the attraction of the 6 cylinder engines which had been successfully adopted by some of the European manufacturers who had discovered that the formula of low geared, high revving engines, driving large bodied cars was a winning one.

The six cylinder cars were to be produced in relatively small numbers compared to the Midgets of the era as they did not generate quite the same affection. Performance wise, although very smooth, they did not give the same exhilaration as the smaller MGs. The first Magnette announced at the 1932 Motor Show was to form an important part of MG history and was the basis for an out-and-out racing model. The K series were to embrace the most renowned MG model of all time the K3 racer, a car that was to bring worldwide fame to the Abingdon factory. This car was powered by a 1087cc KB type, six cylinder engine that gave Cecil Kimber his much desired entry into the 1100cc Class of racing. The chassis was of conventional MG design, although the track, wheelbase and width were all increased over the previous Midgets and Magnas which allowed much more interior space in either open four seat touring form or as a four door pillarless saloon.

In 1933 the Magna range was updated with the introduction of the L type which carried an engine derived from the KB unit This became known as the KC engine and had coil instead of magneto ignition and twin carburettors. The engine was of shorter stroke which at 57mm x 71mm was identical to the racing Midgets of the era. At this time there was a lot of development work going on at Abingdon, particularly in regard to their racing involvement. This development had to be paid for and was ultimately reflected in the prices of the end product and made the already expensive Magnettes even harder to sell. Although the Abingdon expenditure was relatively modest in terms of competition victories, the concentration of effort on this side had been at the expense of fulfilling the market needs. Therefore in 1934, the MG range was slimmed down and the P type was introduced to replace the J2 which at the time was the mainstay of the range, despite serviceability problems with the two bearing crankshaft that had a habit of snapping in two at high engine revs. This new

Midget arrived in February of that year closely followed in March by the new N type range that was to replace the Magnas and introduce some standardisation and rationalisation to the range.

The N types departed for the first time from the standard 'ladder type' frame chassis with the side frame members being wider at the rear than at the front. There was also a new innovation with outrigger members being mounted on Silentbloc rubber bushes. These were fixed to the side and rear of the main chassis and carried the body which resulted in a more comfortable ride. The first N type became designated the NA and was available either as a two seater or four seater open tourer with the usual distinctive slab type petrol tank being disguised behind a very elegant swept tail that incorporated a semi recessed spare wheel. Very soon after its launch, specialist coachbuilders announced their variants of the car. Firstly, Allingham produced a body that resurrected the previously fashionable dicky seat and Carbodies had full factory backing for their Airline Coupé. The Coupé was a very attractive car and Carbodies had certainly proportioned the body well to compliment the NA chassis. It is estimated that only about 7 of these Airlines were produced, making them an extremely rare car. Also a rarity was the ND hybrid which made use of redundant K2 bodies mated to the N type chassis and in similar fashion, surplus K1 pillarless saloon bodies were attached to the N type chassis to form what was known as the KN saloon.

It was a modified version of the KD type engine that was to power the N series. This unit had a displacement of 1271cc and a power output of 56bhp at 5,500rpm. Modifications were fairly extensive involving the cylinder block, cylinder head, inlet manifold, oil lubrication system and clutch. These modifications introduced a 25% power increase over the KD unit on which it was based and gave the N type quite brisk performance. The gearbox was very similar to that used in the L type being non-synchromesh and having a reverse gate. Different ratios however were employed giving lower ratios in first and second and higher cruising ratios in third and top. In 1935 the mechanical specification

of the NA was altered with a close ratio gearbox being fitted whilst body changes included the lowering of the top scuttle and the fitting of forward hinged doors. A slatted radiator similar to that employed on 18/80s and the PB, was fitted to distinguish it from its predecessor. This new version of the N type was configured the NB and was in production for most of 1936 being the last of the overhead camshaft models to be produced before the introduction of the VA one and a half litre model that sported a pushrod overhead valve engine.

The delightful 1935 NA Airline Coupé featured is thought to be one of only four that survive from the original seven that were produced and is owned by Colin Teiche.

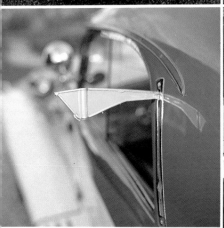
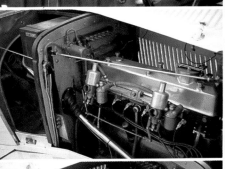

**SPECIFICATION**
Engine: 6 cylinder in line.
Capacity: 1271cc.
Bore & Stroke: 57mm x 83mm
Valve operation: Single overhead camshaft driven through vertical dynamo.
Carburation: Twin semi downdraught SU HV2.
Power Output: 56 bhp at 5,500 rpm.
Gearbox: 4 speed non-synchromesh 'crash' gearbox.
Brakes: 12" drum, front & rear, cable operated.
Clutch: Single dry plate.
Suspension: Half elliptic front & rear with sliding trunnions.
Wheels: Centre lock wire spoke.
Wheelbase: 8' 0".
Track: 3' 9" front and rear.
Number produced: 7
Cost new in 1935: £385.

# NA Magnette Allingham Coupé

The 'N' series of six cylinder cars was introduced in March 1934 not to replace the already popular 'K' series but to compliment the range. Six cylinder cars were very much in vogue in the decade 1925 to 1935 and Cecil Kimber was keen to ensure that MG were in the forefront of the market place with a good varied range of cars on offer to the sports car community. MG were the only car company solely dedicated to the production of sports cars in the early thirties and as such were in a

PLAYER'S CIGARETTES

M.G. MAGNETTE N TYPE

commanding position having built a very good reputation on earlier competition successes. Kimber had always appreciated the sales potential of associating the production cars very closely with the racing models and in 1932 the name "Magnette" was introduced as an identifier for the six cylinder 'K' series cars. This name along with the "Magna" designation became synonymous with success due to the good publicity that ensued all the competition wins and the high racing-biased profile that the MG Car Company maintained during the thirties. The theory of the racing and competition successes boosting sales was a good one and this formula had certainly worked in the early 1930's with Abingdon imparting the impression with enthusiasm, however during 1933 price rises amongst other things had taken their toll on sales. The new 6 cylinder Magnettes were now considered expensive and for some reason did not seem to generate quite the same enthusiasm for the marque as the Midgets of the era. The six cylinder cars were very smooth in their delivery of power although in no way gave the same exhilaration to the driver as the smaller, higher revving J2 Midgets which continued to sell well. During 1933 the Magna range was updated with the introduction of the 'L' type in which was placed an engine derived from the KB Magnette power unit. The 'L' types sold well alongside the 'K' series as they had comparable performance and were considerably cheaper than their stablemates. There was at this time a significant amount of development work going on at Abingdon, particularly with regard to their racing involvement. This development had to be paid for from the profits of the production cars and this was reflected in the prices of the end product. The already expensive Magnettes became even harder to sell and although Abingdon's expenditure was relatively modest in terms of competition victories, the concentration of effort on this side was at the expense of fulfilling the market needs.

In 1934 as a result of cost cutting and in the interests of rationalisation and standardisation, the MG range was slimmed down and the 'P'

type was introduced to replace the J2 in February of that year. The new 'N' type range was to closely follow in March and was destined to replace the Magna range. The 'N' type with its 1271 cc engine was altogether a much "livelier" car than its 6 cylinder predecessors with a 25% increase in power. A modified version of the 'KD' engine was to power the car and it produced 56 bhp at 5,500 rpm. Modifications were fairly extensive and involved the cylinder block, cylinder head, inlet manifold, oil lubrication system and clutch. The gearbox was very similar to that used in the 'L' type being non-synchromesh and of reverse gate. Different ratios were used however giving lower ratios in first and second gear with a higher cruising ratio in third and top gear. The car was also much lighter than its predecessors as the 'N' types departed for the first time from the conventional "ladder type" chassis frame with the side members being wider at the rear than the front.

A new innovative feature was the mounting of the outrigger members on "silentbloc" rubber bushes. These were fixed to the side and rear of the main chassis and carried the body which resulted in a more comfortable ride. The 'N' type or 'NA' as it was designated

was available as a two or four seater with the previously distinctive slab-type petrol tank now disguised behind a stylish swept tail that incorporated a semi-recessed spare wheel. A small

number of cars were built utilising the old 'K2' slab tank bodies and these were designated the 'NK' or more commonly known as the 'ND'. These cars were sold to the sporting enthusiasts and were intended for trials use although in practice the standard two seater was lighter and was actually more successful in competition.

Shortly after the launch, two other body styles were announced and made available through specialist outlets. A popular conversion was the 2/4 seater Allingham Coupé, produced by H.W. Allingham, a fine example of which is the featured car. The flowing coachbuilt lines incorporated a retractable dickey-type seat, this previously fashionable additional seating arrangement was resurrected and very ingeniously set into the tail section of the car. A lid behind the two front seats was normally locked in position giving the impression of a two seater sports car. When the lid was released and pivoted backwards, it revealed the additional seat squab and what was the lid became the back of the seat. Two extra passengers could now be carried in relative comfort. Both the Allingham, whose body was built by Whittingham and Mitchel and another coachbuilt 'N' type Airline Coupé by Carbodies of Coventry carried full Abingdon approval and were listed and promoted in all the factory literature. The normal warranties on the chassis and running gear were extended by M.G. through the coachbuilders to cover the complete car which further endorsed their approval of these distinctive coachbuilt versions.

JK 4389 is thought to be one of only three that survive complete from the original eleven that were produced by H.W. Allingham (a chassis only is also known to survive). This very attractive and rare 'NA' M.G. was built in 1934 and is in the proud ownership of Robin Mace.

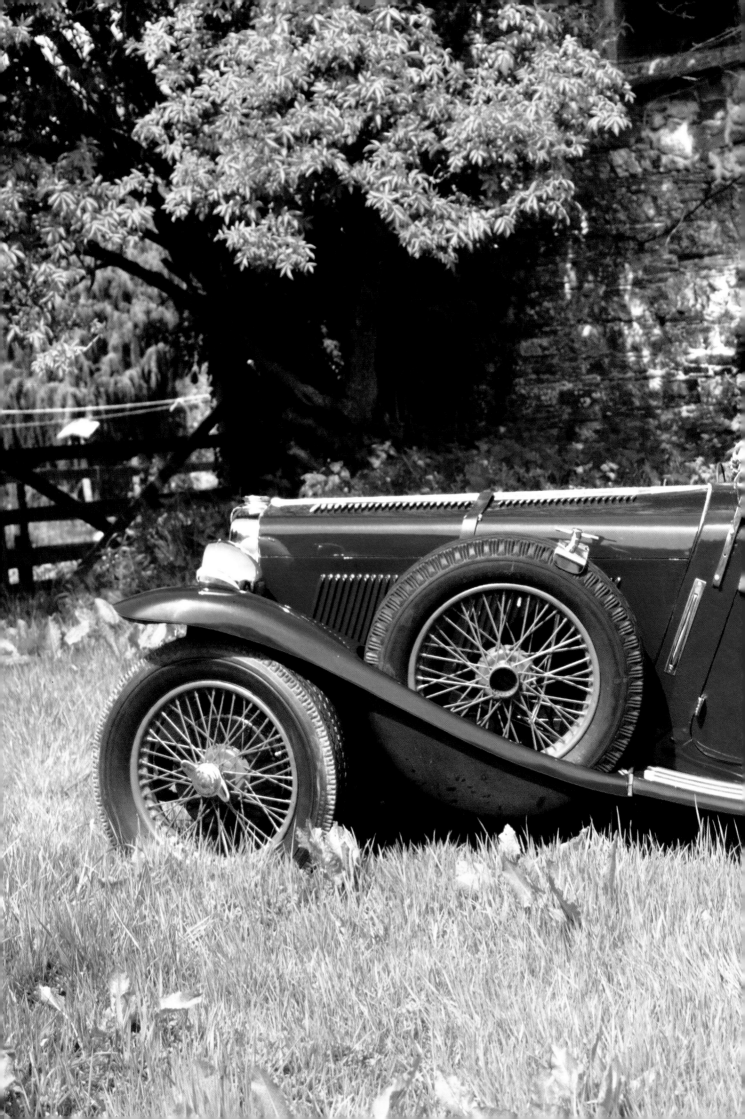

# NA Magnette Allingham Coupé

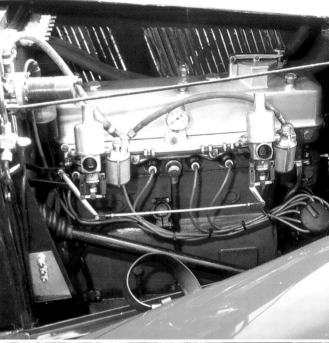

SPECIFICATION
Engine: 6 Cylinder in line.
Capacity: 1271cc.
Bore & Stroke: 57mm x 83mm.
Valve operation: Single overhead camshaft driven through vertical dynamo.
Carburation: Twin semi-downdraught SU HV2
Power Output: 56bhp @ 5,500rpm.
Gearbox: 4 speed non-synchromesh 'crash' gearbox.
Brakes:
12" drum front & rear, cable operated.
Clutch: Single dry plate.
Chassis: Steel channel with tubular cross members.
Suspension: Half elliptic front & rear with sliding trunnions.
Wheels: Centre lock Rudge Whitworth wire spoke.
Wheelbase: 8'0".
Track: 3'9" front & rear..
Numbers produced: Believed to be 11.
Cost new in 1935: £330

# NB Magnette

It was in 1932 that Cecil Kimber introduced the Magnette name to a new series of cars. The 18/80 was nearing the end of its useful production life and it was at the 1932 Motor Show that a new 6 cylinder car was announced, designated the 'K' Series following on in logical sequence from the J' types. This new model

was to be an important basis for a new racing car to compete in the 1100cc Class and was powered by a 1087cc straight six engine. The chassis was of conventional MG design although the track, wheelbase and width were all increased over the previous Midgets and Magnas allowing more interior space in either open four seat touring form or four door pillarless saloon. The engine was known as the KA based closely on the Wolseley Hornet and was deemed underpowered for the long wheelbase K1 and short wheelbase K2, so very soon after these two models had gone into production a more powerful KB type engine was made available. This was put into the open tourers as they were considered to be more worthy of the extra power, whilst the KA type engine was retained for use in the more sedate saloons. The Magnette range generally were offered with a non-synchromesh 'crash' gearbox although a Wilson type pre-selector gearbox was available as an option. There was a racing model of the 'K' Series dubbed the K3 which was thought to be the real reason for the production of the entire 'K' range as Cecil Kimber could not justify the manufacture of a racing model on its own at the time.

During 1933 the Magna range was updated with the introduction of the 'L' type in which was placed an engine derived from the KB Magnette power unit. This became known as the KC type with coil ignition and twin carbu-

rettors. The engine had a shorter stroke of 57mm x 71mm which was identical to the racing Midgets of the era. The 'K' Magnette was considerably more expensive than the Magna so an even more powerful engine was produced by enlarging the unit to 1271 cc and increasing the stroke thus making it a genuine top of the range model. This new engine was known as the KD type and it produced 25% more power than the original unit and was coupled to the now standard pre-selector gearbox. There was at this time, a lot of development work going on at Abingdon, and there was huge involvement in racing also. This was reflected in a general rise in the prices of the end product which made the already expensive Magnettes even harder to sell. Although the company's expenditure was relatively modest in terms of the racing victories, the concentration of effort on this side had been at the expense of fulfilling the market needs. So in 1934 the range was reduced and the P type was introduced to replace the J2 which at that time was the mainstay of the range despite the unserviceability of the two bearing crankshaft which generally broke in two when revving the engine at peak speeds. This new Midget arrived on the market in February of that year sporting a new 3 bearing 847cc engine that was far sturdier than that used by its predecessor. In March the 'N' types were introduced to replace the Magnas and gain some standardisation and rationalisation of the range.

The 'N' type Magnette was important because it was MGs first departure from the familiar standard type ladder frame chassis with the side members being wider at the rear than the front. There was also a new innovation with outrigger members mounted on 'Silentbloc' rubber bushes. These were fixed to the side and rear of the main chassis and carried the body. The 'N' or 'NA' as it was known was available with a choice of either two or four seater bodies and the previously distinctive slab type petrol tank was now disguised behind a very elegant swept tail that incorporated a semi-recessed spare wheel. Shortly after its launch two other body styles were announced by specialist coachbuilders. One was made by Allingham and this body resurrected and incorporated the previously fashionable dickey seat. A few Airline fixed-head coupes were also produced at this time, which were most attractive. It is estimated that about 12 of each model were made, making them

extremely rare indeed. Also rare is the ND hybrid which was made from redundant K2 bodies fitted to the N type chassis and in similar fashion, surplus K1 pillarless saloon bodies were mated to the N type chassis to form what was known as the KN saloon .

The engine used in the 'N' type was developed from the KD unit previously mentioned with a displacement of 1271cc and power output of 56bhp at 5,500rpm. Modifications were fairly extensive involving the cylinder block, cylinder head, inlet manifold, oil lubrication system and clutch. These modifications saw a 25% power output increase over the KD unit and this gave the 'N' type fairly good performance. The gearbox was similar to that used in the 'L' type, being non-synchromesh and reverse gate but with different gear ratios having two low starting gears and two high ratio cruising gears. In 1935 the mechanical specification of the 'N' type was altered with a closer ratio gearbox being fitted and there were also improvements to the bodywork with a revised lowered scuttle and forward hinged doors. A slatted radiator was employed to distinguish it from the 'NA' and was similar to that used on the 18/80s and the PB. This model was configured the 'NB' by Abingdon and was in production for most of 1936 being the last of the overhead cam MGs to be produced before being finally replaced by the one and a half litre, four cylinder VA model with its pushrod overhead valve engine.

There was in 1934 a racing version of the 'N' type produced known as the 'NE' and it was specially developed for the 1934 TT race in which superchargers were banned for the first time, this was perhaps in an attempt to break MGs previous dominance of the race. Against all odds, the 'NE' won the race on handicap, being faster than all other finishers, some of them sporting four and a half litre engines. Of the six 'NE' models produced, some were used successfully throughout 1936 by the Cream Crackers Trials Team. However by 1935 the era of the small six cylinder engine was coming to a close with large capacity four cylinder engines, mounted on rubber blocks, providing far better torque characteristics. This was the end of an era for MG with rationalization on the horizon, brought in by the Nuffield organisation which was to change the MG range dramatically. The featured car is owned by Ron Saville.

# NB Magnette

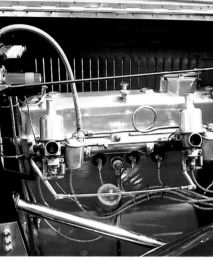

**Specification:**
Engine: 6 cylinder in line
Capacity: 1271cc
Bore & Stroke: 57mm x 83mm
Valve Operation: Single overhead camshaft driven through vertical dynamo
Carburation: Twin semi-downdraught SUs
Power Output: 56bhp @ 5,500rpm
Gearbox: 4 speed non-synchromesh 'crash' gearbox
Brakes: 12″ drum front and rear, cable operated.
Clutch: Dry plate clutch
Suspension: Half elliptic front and rear with sliding trunnions
Wheels: Centre lock wire spoke
Wheelbase: 8′0″
Track: 3′9″ front and rear
Max speed: 80mph
Acceleration: 0-60mph: 22.7 secs
Number produced (NA & NB): 690
Price new: £335

# ND Magnette

The MG Car Company were in a very commanding position in the early thirties, being the only concern that were dedicated solely to the manufacture of sports cars. They had earned tremendous recognition and built a reputation second to none on their unfailing successes in racing and competition, particularly with small capacity engines. Cecil Kimber had always recognised the sales potential of associating the production cars very closely with the racing models and in 1932 a new series of cars designated K Type, was introduced into the model range which encompassed a variant built specifically for racing. Kimber knew he could not justify the manufacture of a racing model on its own and it is thought that he cleverly used the other K series cars as a smokescreen for the out and out racing model, the K3. It was at this time that the name Magnette was introduced to the series and it was this name that heralded the arrival of the "Light Sixes" as they became known.

The impression generated by Abingdon was that the racing successes had boosted demand for their cars, but if the truth be known, sales were less than buoyant during 1933 and in fact price rises had taken their toll on sales. The new 6 cylinder Magnettes were considered very expensive and somehow did not generate quite the same affection for the marque as the Midgets of the era. The K series pillarless saloon version was considered noisy, cramped and underpowered and thus did not sell in great numbers. The 6 cylinder L series cars did fair slightly better and were on sale alongside the K types, with only the L type Continental Coupé, better known as Kimbers' Folly, suffering from a disastrous lack of interest. The 6 cylinder cars were very smooth in their delivery of power although in no way gave the same exhilaration to the driver as the smaller J2 Midgets which continued to sell steadily although suffering from serviceability problems with premature failure of the crankshaft.

Racing development was costly and although Abingdon's expenditure was quite modest in relation to the number of competition victories,

the concentration of effort on this side had been at the expense of fulfilling the market needs. A directive from Sir William Morris to restrict expenditure on racing was met with dismay and there were also restrictions imposed on Kimber to buy as many of the components needed for MG from within the Morris group. In the latter half of 1933, this led to the severing of the long standing relationship for the supply of bodies from Carbodies with them now being made by Morris Bodies Branch. Further directives demanded a slimming down of the range of cars offered and therefore in February 1934 the MG range was changed by the introduction of a new P type Midget to replace the J2 Midget. This was

closely followed in March with the introduction of the N type Magnettes which were to replace the Magnas and at the same time inject some standardisation and rationalisation into the MG range. It is worthy of note that at the 1934 Motor Show the K series was still promoted alongside the new N types and the main reason for this being the glut of saloon and open 4 seater bodies held in stock.

The best features of previous models were incorporated into the N types and it was evident that a lot of time had been spent in

designing improvements into this new range which consisted of either 2 or 4 seat open tourers or Allingham coachbuilt 2/4 seater bodies or the option of the delightful Airline Coupé. There was also a pillarless saloon which was designated the KN which was simply the old K saloon with the new N type engine and a hybrid ND two seater which made use of redundant K2 slabtank bodies mated to the new N type chassis. Only 24 of these were built. Finally there was a special racing version, of which only 6 were made, designated the NE racer. This car was developed specially to compete in the 1934 TT races in which superchargers were banned for the first time. This move was seen as an attempt to break MGs previous dominance of the race, however the NE won the race on handicap against stiff competition from some of the larger 4.5 litre cars.

The engine of the N type was a modified version of the KD power unit of 1271 cc and with a respectable power output of 56.6 bhp @ 5,500 rpm. Both the cylinder head and block were changed together with modifications to the inlet manifolding, oil lubrication system and clutch. These modifications gave the new unit a 25% increase in power over the original KD engine and gave the N type quite brisk performance. The gearbox changed from pre-selector to manual non-synchromesh and was very similar to that used in the L type Magnas. The gear selector utilised a reverse gate as in the Magna but the ratios were changed to give lower starting ratios in first and second and higher cruising ratios in third and fourth. The chassis frame was quite different from the earlier cars and departed for the first time from the standard "ladder" type frame. It tapered, being wider at the rear than the front and also for the first time the bodies were mounted on Silentbloc rubber bushes. These were fixed to the side and the rear of the main chassis and altogether produced a far more comfortable ride. However the days of the high revving overhead camshaft engines were numbered and although production of the "Light Sixes" continued on into 1936, the N type was certainly the last of these. Larger capacity four cylinder pushrod overhead valve engines mounted on rubber blocks were soon to give better and more refined performance with enhanced torque characteristics and appeared for the first time in 1936 in the VA 1.5 litre saloon. The beautiful 1934 ND Magnette featured this month is owned by Philip Bayne-Powell.

*Big cars and little cars came to the trial that day. Split fractions of a second counted. Streaking up, cleanly, scientifically, superbly, roared the astonishing M.G. Magnettes. Best performance of the day again! Magnettes first—once more! Such is the courage and the character of the car you can buy this very day— the M.G. It is a car which will be a fresh delight each day you drive.*

*Buy a car made in the United Kingdom.*

M.G. Magnette 'N' Type 6-cyl. 1287 cc., from £280. M.G. Midget 'PB' Type 4-cyl. 939 cc., from £222
M.G. Midget 'P' Type 4-cyl. 847 cc., from £199 10s. Dunlop : Triplex : Prices ex works

THE M.G. CAR COMPANY LIMITED, ABINGDON-ON-THAMES, BERKSHIRE
SOLE EXPORTERS: M.I.R. LTD. COWLEY OXFORD ENGLAND

# ND MAGNETTE

## SPECIFICATION

Engine: 6 cylinder in-line
Capacity: 1271 cc
Bore & Stroke: 57mm x 83mm
Valve operation: Single overhead
camshaft driven through vertical
dynamo
Carburation: Single SU carburettor
running through Marshall
supercharger
Power output: 56 bhp @ 5,500 rpm
(standard car) approx 75-80 bhp
with supercharger
Gearbox: 4 speed non-synchromesh
'crash' gearbox
Brakes: 12" drum front & rear, cable
operated
Clutch: Single dry plate
Suspension: Half elliptic front & rear
with sliding trunnions
Wheels: Centre-lock wire spoke
Wheelbase: 8' 0"
Track: 3' 9" front & rear
Number produced: 24

# PA Midget Airline Coupé

Launched in March 1934, the P type Midget was a direct replacement for the J2. The J series power unit had been dogged with crankshaft problems, particularly when any attempts were made at raising the state of tune. The simple two bearing crank was very prone to breaking and was a source of embarrassment to the MG engineers, it did not mean however that the car was necessarily unreliable or that every crankshaft was likely to break under normal running conditions. What it did mean was that limitations were imposed, particularly in competition use. Even the fully counterbalanced J4 crankshaft had restrictions on the supercharger pressure that could be applied to the engine before serious crank whiplash set in. The J2 had detectable distortion of the crank with only modest compression ratios applied. The logical next step in the development of the Midget power units was to insert a centre bearing to alleviate the aforementioned problems, already the design of the L and K type engines incorporated adequate intermediate main bearings and the diameter of the camshaft had been increased by comparison with previous types. These 1100 cc, 6 cylinder engines had proved that they could withstand high crankshaft speeds for long periods with little sign of stress, therefore the engine designers used this engine as the basis for the new P type power unit. They simply 'cut out' cylinders four and five and retained all the other desirable components. This new engine was to be the basis of the power unit for the P, Q and R type cars.

'Autocar' magazine road tested the P type in November 1934 and reported "This latest model is a marked improvement in all respects over its forerunners". Sales literature produced by Abingdon claimed "In all there are over one hundred new and improved features". With good reports in the motoring press it was no surprise that the car sold well. Serious production of the car had started in January 1934 which meant that there was no wait for the car, very soon over 200 vehicles a month were coming off the line at Abingdon. The first cars produced were all two seaters and following its predecessor the J2 had its wheels painted to match the car's interior, this was soon dropped in favour of aluminium paint. P types were available in three distinctive duo-tone paint schemes and each one came with matching upholstery. They were: Ulster Green/Dublin Green, Oxford Blue/Cambridge Blue and Carmine Red and Saratoga Red. The most popular single colour scheme however was Black, closely followed by Green and then Red followed by Blue. Some cars were produced in primer only to allow the prospective owner to have the car painted to his choice and for an extra ten guineas the owner could specify the factory to complete the car in any colour leather or bodywork he so desired. The level of standard equipment described in the sales brochure of the time indicated that it was "all the usual equipment that sportsmen demand - supplemented by the following new extras: Easily accessible tool accommodation; non-reflecting fascia board; new revolution counter; chromium plated long range headlamps; new seat adjustment; dual arm electric windscreen

wiper: stop and tail lamp: improved hood and side screen curtains; new fold-flat windscreen with toughened non-discolourable Triplex safety glass".

Both front and rear axles were similar to the J type but the chassis frame was marginally longer and made of heavier gauge steel. The transmission was strengthened and improved to withstand the increased engine power output and stresses imposed by competition work and a new design heavy duty clutch was

employed to cater for the rigorous stops and starts on hill climbs and sprints. A four speed non-synchromesh gearbox with a low ratio first gear for competition purposes transferred the power to specially strengthened rear axle with a four star differential. J4/L type 12 inch diameter brake drums replaced the previously used 8 inch variety. This move gave far greater and safer braking. Hartford friction dampers were fitted to the front of the car and transversely mounted hydraulic spring compensated shock absorbers at the rear gave good suspension and a comfortable ride over most surfaces. With its beautifully smooth engine the P type very soon had many supporters with superb handling the car could be pushed hard for miles on end with no adverse affect. Performance was brisk but substantially the same as its predecessor the J type due to its increased weight. There was soon a demand for more power so after the PA had been in production for 18 months a new version appeared dubbed the PB. This sported an engine that was 10% larger attained by boring out from 57mm to 60mm. Little else was changed and this increased the power output from 35 bhp at 5.600 rpm to 43.3 bhp at 5,500 rpm. The 939cc engine coupled to a close ration gearbox transformed the car. Other changes included a slatted grille instead of the honeycomb type, a quick-release fuel filler cap was now standard on the two seater versions. The dashboard was to feature a burr walnut fascia to replace the now banned American Sequoia redwood veneer. The rev counter was changed and a speedometer with a mileage trip meter replaced the P types centre panel. A 30 mph warning light was also introduced at this time.

The PA was available either as a two or four seater with no saloon version offered, however a fixed head coupe was offered on the P type chassis by some specialist coachbuilders such as H W Allingham of London, University Motors (who were main MG agents) and Cresta Motors of Worthing. By far the most popular of these conversions was that undertaken by H W Allingham and called the Airline Coupé. Such a car is the beautiful 1934 example featured and it is one of only two in the UK at present. Very few of these stunningly attractive cars were made because they were considered fairly expensive at the time and larger standard cars could be bought for about the same price. When introduced the P type two seater sold for £220 compared to £240 for the four seater version. The Airline Coupé was offered at £290. The Airline was launched at the Autumn 1934 Motor Show and proved something of a sensation with its graceful flowing bodyline. A total of 28 Coupés were made on the PA chassis with 14 being produced as PB's. Only about 12 cars in total worldwide are thought to exist and the featured car, in concours condition, must undoubtably be the finest example of this highly desirable and rare MG. The car is owned by John Shute.

# PA
# AIRLINE COUPÉ

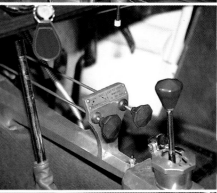

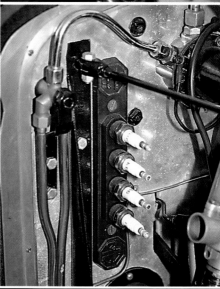

## SPECIFICATION

Engine: 4 cylinder in line. Bore & stroke: 57mm x 83mm.

Capacity: 847cc

Carburation: Twin SU HV2

Valve operation: Single overhead camshaft.

Power output: 36 bhp @ 5,500 rpm.

Gearbox: 4 speed non-synchromesh.

Clutch: Single dry plate.

Brakes: Mechanically operated, 12" drum front & rear.

Wheels & tyres: 19 x 4" knock-on centre-lock wire wheel.

Track: 3' 6"

Wheelbase: 7' 3.3"

Price new in 1934: £290

Number built: PA Airline; 28. PB Airline; 14.

Total all variants: 2,500 from 1934-36.

The P type Midget was launched in March 1934 as the replacement for the J2. It is well recognised that the P type had similarities with

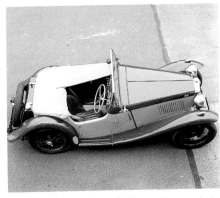

previous Magnas and Magnettes and its parentage derived from the M and J types Autocar magazine roadtested the P type in November of that year and reported "This latest model is a marked improvement in all respects over its forerunners". Sales literature produced by Abingdon claimed. "In all there are over one hundred new and improved features". With good reports in the motoring press it was no surprise that the car sold well, with serious production starting at the end of January 1934, over two hundred cars a month were coming off the production lines.

The P type was fitted with an all new 847cc engine, with three main bearings supporting the rigid crankshaft. This allowed higher engine revolutions to be employed with safety. An improved Tecalemit oil lubrication and filtering system was a welcome addition to the engine. This system had two filters, one externally and the other was a gauze mesh in the sump, both of which ensured thorough filtering of the oil, thus prolonging the life of the crankshaft and cylinder bores. A "smooth flow" cylinder head with inlet ports on one side and exhaust on the other had an overhead camshaft.

The transmission was strengthened and improved to withstand the increased engine power output and stresses imposed by competition work and a new design heavy duty clutch was employed to cater for the rigorous stops and starts on sprints and hill climbs. A four speed non-synchromesh gearbox with a low ratio first gear for competition purposes transferred the power to a specially strengthened back axle with a four star differential. Twelve inch diameter brake drums replaced the previously used eight inch variety. This move gave far greater braking efficiency. Hartford friction dampers were fitted to the front of the car and transversally mounted

hydraulic spring compensated shock absorbers at the rear gave good suspension and a comfortable ride over most surfaces.

The level of standard equipment described in the sales brochure of the time indicated that it was "all the usual equipment that sportsmen demand - supplemented by the following new extras: Easily accessible tool accommodation. non-reflecting fascia board. new revolution counter; chromium plated long range headlamps; new seat adjustment; dual arm electric windscreen wiper; stop and tail lamp; improved hood and side curtains; and new fold flat windscreen with toughened non-discolourable Triplex safety glass."

The first cars produced were all two seaters and following its predecessor the J2 had its wheels painted to match the car's interior, this was soon dropped in favour of aluminium paint. P types were available in three distinctive duo-tone paint schemes, each one came with matching upholstery. The feature car is painted in Ulster Green and Dublin Green, other options were: Oxford Blue and Cambridge Blue and Carmine Red and Saratoga Red. The most popular single colour scheme however was Black, closely followed by Green and then Red followed by Blue. Some cars were produced in primer only to allow the prospective owner to have the car painted to his choice and for an extra ten guineas the owner could specify the factory to complete the car in any colour leather or bodywork he so desired.

Most of the design knowledge gained from previous involvement in production car trials and racing proved invaluable to the production of the P type. The chassis was far sturdier than the J type and the body was less angular and had more flowing lines. Two variations were available with either a two or four seater version coming direct from the factory, however a fixed head coupe was offered on the P type chassis by specialist coachbuilders such as H W Allingham of London, University Motors (who were main MG agents) and Cresta Motors of Worthing. The most popular of these conversions was undoubtedly the Airline Coupé by H W Allingham but very few of these attractive cars were produced because they were considered fairly expensive and larger standard cars could be bought for about the same price. When introduced the P type two seater sold for £220 compared to £240 for the four seater version. The Airline Coupé was offered at £290.

The P type was never intended as a racing

model, unlike many of its predecessors, however it was seen on the circuits and in 1935 a three car team of P types was entered in the 24 hour Le Mans race. The team was managed by George Eyston and consisted of six ladies affectionately known as "The Dancing Daughters" although they attracted much publicity, they did not fair particularly well against opposition from Singer's 972cc sports car. The Singers took 1st. 3rd and 4th places. This along with other factors prompted Abingdon to produce a more powerful model, to be designated the PB which was introduced in 1935. The engine capacity was increased to 939cc to give more power and a close ratio gearbox was fitted. Other changes included a slatted grille instead of the honeycomb type, a quick release petrol filler cap was now standard on the two seater versions. The dashboard was to feature a burr walnut fascia to replace the banned American Sequoia redwood veneer. The rev counter was changed and a speedometer with a mileage trip meter replaced the P type's centre panel. A 30 mph warning light was also introduced at this time. The original P type was discontinued in favour of the new model although it was still catalogued at a substantially reduced price. This move failed to sell the remaining stocks and 27 P types were converted to PB models by the end of 1935. Production of the PB finally ceased in February 1936 with only 525 being produced. A total of 2,500 P types left Abingdon between 1933 and 1936. The immaculate 1934 PA featured is owned by pre-war MG specialist. Roger Thomas.

# PA

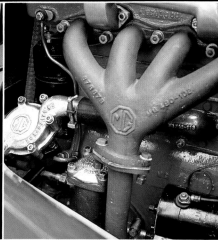

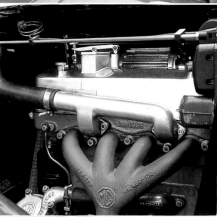

**Specification:**
Engine
No. of cylinder: 4 in line
Bore and stroke: 57mm x 83mm
Capacity: 847cc
Valve operation: Single overhead camshaft
RAC rating: 8 hp
Approx power output: 36 bhp at 5500 rpm in standard form
Gearbox: 4 speed non-synchromesh
Brakes: Mechanical 12'' drum operated by cable
Wheels and Tyres: 19 x 4.00'' knock on centre lock wire wheel
Track: 3' 6''
Wheelbase: 7' 3.5''
Length: 10' 11''
Weight: 13 cwt 2 qtrs
Performance
Max speed: 76.27 mph (windscreen lowered), 69.23 mph (windscreen raised)
Acceleration: 0-60 mph 32.3 secs
MPG: approx 35.
Number built: 1973 (although 27 converted to PB are not included)
Cost new in 1934: £222

# Q Type Midget

Produced solely for competition purposes only eight Q Types were built by Abingdon at the latter end of 1934. Aspiring race drivers were offered the Q type with the same bore and stroke of the earlier 750 cc P Types. The same block and head were employed, however a special crank and push rods were used which were specially strengthened and latterly employed on most of the overhead cam racing engines. The chassis was 8" longer in the wheelbase and 3" wider in the track than its predecessor the racing J4, in fact the development of the Q Type came from an amalgamation of several previous models including the N and P Type MGs. It incorporated the N type steering gear and brakes although larger special drums were used. The Q Type had a pre

In a mild state of tune the 746 cc engine could produce well in excess of 110 bhp and in its final racing form in 1936 it produced nearly 147 bhp at 7500 rpm. This equated to a figure of 200 bhp per 1000 cc and was higher than any other racing engine in the world at that time.

The engine development by MG engineers was far in advance of chassis design and when the Q Type proved too fast for its chassis radical steps were taken by the design teams for a revolutionary new design of chassis, thus evolved the lightweight backbone chassis with all independent suspension and hydraulic shock absorbers, which was ultimately to be used on the R Type race car. Bodywork of the Q type was very similar to the 1934 K3 Magnette, but the 19 gallon fuel tank

was enclosed and incorporated inside the rear tail panelling. The Q Type could be purchased in 1934 for a very reasonable £550 giving excellent value against competitors utilising huge 12 or 16 cylinder engines with lower power outputs. The Mercedes or Auto Unions were easily two or three times the cost of the MG and sometimes less reliable. The car had qualified successes in many racing and sprinting events and a highly modified Q Type driven by George Harvey-Noble in 1937 broke the Brooklands Outer Circuit Class H record at an amazing speed of 122.4 mph.

selector gearbox as used on the K3, but differed in as much as it had a special clutch which was designed to slip automatically above a certain torque figure, which avoided the possibility of damage to the N Type rear axle.

A high pressure Zoller supercharger was introduced at this time and mated to the Q type engine, this increased the manifold pressures to at least two and a half atmospheres and the resulting power output was quite remarkable.

# Q Type Midget

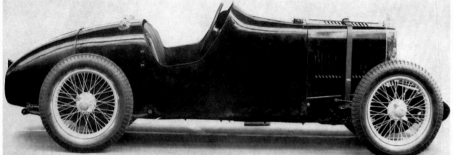

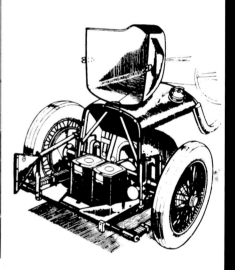

SPECIFICATION

**Engine**
No of cylinders: 4
Bore and Stroke: 57mm x 73mm
Capacity: 746cc
Power output: 113 bhp at 7,200 rpm
Valve operation: Overhead camshaft driven through vertical dynamo
MPG: approx 8
Gearbox: 4 speed ENV pre-selector with overload clutch
Carburation: Single SU HVB through Zoller supercharger
Chassis: Steel channel side members with tubular cross members
Suspension: Half elliptic springs front and rear with sliding trunnions
Wheels: Centre lock Rudge Whitworth wire spoke
Brakes: 12 inch drum mechanically operated by cable
Steering: Bishop cam, worm and peg
Track: 3' 9" front and rear
Wheelbase: 7' 10"
Number built: 8

# SA 2 Litre Saloon

The MG SA was launched at the 1935 Motor Show and this elegant saloon was the first all new model to be introduced since the merger with Morris Motors in July 1935. It was launched alongside another new model, the PB Midget and a revised version of the N type Magnette, but everyone's attention was turned to the SA. This brand new car was a shock to the MG fraternity as it was a car of such huge proportions compared to the previous Abingdon offerings and was to be the largest MG to date. Many enthusiasts refused to recognise the SA as a genuine MG choosing to forget the fact that some of the earlier Magnettes were not exactly small cars. To understand the reasoning behind the launch of this luxury sports saloon, we need to look back to early 1935 and the revolution that swept through Abingdon. Leonard Lord was appointed as the new managing director of the MG Car Company when Nuffield sold the concern to Morris Motors in July 1935. Virtually overnight all racing activities and developments were ceased and although Cecil Kimber remained at Abingdon, there was little that he could do without the consent of Lord. Initially Lord said that he did not want to produce any more MG sports cars as they interfered with his plans to streamline the organisation. However Cecil Kimber still retained a lot of influence and he managed to gain enough support to eventually change Lord's mind. The end result of this disagreement between Kimber and Lord was the production of the MG Two Litre SA Saloon first announced in October 1935.

Lord felt that all that was necessary to sell a Wolseley at an inflated price was to put an MG radiator on it. This thought was rapidly dispelled by Kimber and his supporters and Kimber was allowed to design a new body for the Wolseley chassis. This he did with great success, producing a very attractive well proportioned body and at a mere £375 for the saloon version it was attractively priced as well. It was exceptional value for money particularly when compared to its predecessor the KN Magnette at £399. Other coachwork which included a four seat tourer and the handsome Tickford Coupé followed later. The pleasing appearance of the coachbuilt body was subsequently adopted by some of England's leading coachbuilders, one of note was Mulliner Park Ward. In terms of luxury, internal appointments and overall appeal, the SA stood favourable comparison with many other similar cars of the era. Sadly the car suffered from the inefficiencies that Leonard Lord was trying to get rid of, with the SA going through numerous changes of components, in order to take advantage of the standard items utilised by Wolseley. The production of the car was inevitably delayed through too many people being involved in the decisions surrounding the use of components, production procedures and the general inflexibility of the Nuffield group as a whole.

The SA model was aimed at the larger luxury car market. Based on the Wolseley Super Six, this graceful sports saloon was intended to be a prestige model that would enhance the Company image and move away from the stark and somewhat basic sports cars that had made MG famous. Certainly insurance companies welcomed this departure as there was considerable disapproval previously over the sporting image and hefty premiums were often imposed. This fact was no doubt considered by the Nuffield organisation as they invested heavily in this new luxury sports saloon. The MG purists were however most displeased with the SA as the familiar MG chassis was dispensed with, being substituted with a heavy conventional box-section Wolseley based variety. Gone also was the overhead camshaft engine, which was replaced with a Wolseley Super Six 2 litre pushrod operated unit. The familiar cable operated brakes were replaced with Lockheed hydraulic type, a system that Kimber did not favour at all, maintaining that the old style cable brakes were far more dependable. The prototype had pressed steel bolt-on type wheels instead of the knock-on

wires and as a final insult a synchromesh gearbox with a long unwieldy gearlever was fitted.

The SA had its biggest setback just ten days before the launch of the model was due, when a new sporting saloon was announced by SS Cars of Coventry. MG had never considered this company to be any threat to them in the past, as they were not producing cars to compete in the same market sector. SS also did not have any competition successes worthy of note, however, this new car, the first to bear the Jaguar name, was a far more serious rival. William Lyons, the owner of SS cars was a brilliant designer from the same mould as Kimber, he also made all the major decisions, which meant that the Jaguar SS went straight into production, unlike the floundering Nuffield group which took until early 1936 to decide on the specification and supply the parts for the SA. With the initial publicity long since forgotten, it was over 6 months

since the introduction of the model before the MG Two Litre went into full production. This delay was due also to Abingdon trying to uprate the specification to improve its standing against the Jaguar. The car initially had a 2062 cc engine and this was increased to 2288 cc to match the Jaguars 2663 cc unit. Normally this sort of alteration to the specification would have taken a matter of days when Abingdon were dealing direct with suppliers and were doing their own design work. It took months for the Morris engines division to change the specification as they saw it as a relatively unimportant job. As a direct result many disillusioned customers, over 500 in all, who had been waiting for their cars, changed their orders to the Jaguar SS which was ready for immediate delivery.

Other changes implemented were the replacement of the original bolt-on wheels with centrelock wire wheels but even once production had started in earnest, there were continual changes in specification, which made a mockery of the so-called Nuffield efficiency. These changes could only be attributed to faulty initial design of the components, eventually even the complete chassis frame was modified. By the time of the 1936 Motor Show, circumstances dictated a price rise with the saloon now costing £389 and the Charlesworth open tourer at £385. The Tickford Coupé was introduced at £415. Early in 1937, the engine capacity was changed yet again to 2322 cc, probably to comply with Nuffield standardisation of models and there was little if any improvement in performance as a result. The performance could be described as adequate rather than exhilarating, with the car weighing in at almost a ton and a half and with only 75.3 bhp available, acceleration could only compare to its 18/80 forerunners. The SA did however have a genuine top speed of nearly 85 mph and could sustain a cruising speed all day long of 70 mph plus. The 1936 SA Saloon featured this forms part of the fine collection of MG cars owned by John Shute.

# SA

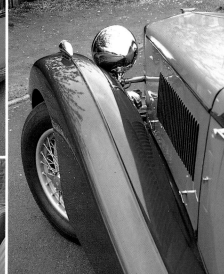

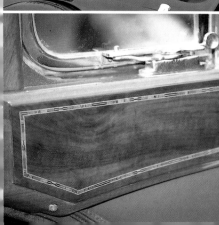

SPECIFICATION:
Engine:
Type: Water cooled in line
Number of cylinders: 6
Bore and Stroke: Early; 69mm x 102mm. Late; 69.5mm x 102mm
Capacity: Early; 2288cc. Late; 2322cc
Valve operation: Pushrod overhead valve.
Compression ratio: approx 6.5:1
Carburation: Twin direct downdraught horizontal SU's
Power output: 75.3 bhp at 4,300 rpm
Clutch: Wet cork
Gearbox: Manual 4 speed crash box on early cars. Part synchro on later cars.
Chassis: Twin side members with cross members.
Wheelbase: 10' 3''
Track: 4' 5⅜'' front and rear
Suspension: Front; half elliptic springs with beam axle
Rear; half elliptic springs, live axle
Brakes: Lockwood hydraulic front and rear with 12'' drums
Performance: Maximum speed: 85 mph
Fuel consumption: approx 17 mpg
Price in 1936: £415
Number Built: 2738 (includes saloon, open tourer and Tickford)

# SA Tickford Coupé

The MG SA was launched at the 1935 Motor Show alongside another new model, the PB Midget. Also on display was a revised version of the N type Magnette, but everyones attention was turned to the SA. This totally new car was a shock to the MG fraternity as it was a car of such huge proportions compared to the previous Abingdon offerings. Many enthusiasts complained that this was not a real MG, forgetting that some of the earlier Magnettes were not exactly small cars. The reasoning behind the launch of this luxury sports saloon was due in part to the revolution that swept through Abingdon in early 1935. The new Managing Director of the MG Car Company was Leonard Lord, he was appointed when Nuffield sold the concern to Morris Motors in July 1935. Almost overnight all racing activities and developments were ceased and although Cecil Kimber remained at Abingdon, there was little that he could do without the consent of Lord. Alarmingly, Lord said that he did not want to produce any more MG sports cars as they interfered with his plans to streamline the organisation, thankfully Cecil Kimber still retained a lot of influence and he managed to gain enough support to eventually change Lord's mind. The product of this conflict between Kimber and Lord was the introduction of the MG Two Litre first announced in October 1935.

Designated the SA model and based on the Wolseley Super Six, it was far bigger than any MG ever produced before. This graceful sports saloon was aimed at the luxury car market and it was intended to be a model that would enhance the Company image and move away from the somewhat basic sports cars that had made MG famous. Insurance companies welcomed this departure as there was considerable disapproval previously over the sporting image and expensive premiums were often imposed. This fact was no doubt considered by the Nuffield organisation as they invested heavily in this new luxury sports saloon. MG purists were most displeased with the SA as the familiar MG chassis had been dispensed with, a heavy conventional box-section Wolseley based variety had replaced it.

Gone also was the over-head camshaft engine which was substituted with a Wolseley Super Six 2 litre pushrod operated unit. The aged cable operated brakes were replaced with Lockheed hydraulic type, a system that Kimber did not favour at all, maintaining that the old style cable brakes were far more dependable. The prototype emerged with pressed steel bolt-on type wheels instead of the knock-on wires and as a final insult a synchromesh gearbox with a long unwieldy gearlever was fitted.

Lord misguidedly thought that he could sell a Wolseley at an inflated price by putting an MG radiator on it. This thought was rapidly dispelled by Kimber and his supporters and Kimber was allowed to design a new body for the Wolseley chassis. He soon produced a very appealing,

well proportioned body and at a mere £375 for the saloon version it was attractively priced as well. It was exceptional value for money particularly when compared to its predecessor the KN Magnette at £399. Other coachwork options which included a four seat tourer and the handsome Tickford Coupé featured followed later. Coachbuilt bodies were subsequently adopted by some of England's leading coachbuilders, one of note was Mulliner Park Ward. In terms of luxury internal appointments and overall appeal the SA stood favourable comparison with many other similar cars of the era. Sadly the car suffered from the very inefficiencies and inflexibility that Leonard Lord was trying to get rid of. The SA went through numerous changes of components in order to take advantage of the standard items utilised by Wolseley. There were many production setbacks with inevitable delays through too many people being involved in the decisions surrounding the use of components and various production procedures.

Just ten days before the launch a new sporting saloon was announced by SS Cars of Coventry, which was quite a bombshell to Kimber. He had never considered this company to be any threat as they were not producing cars to compete in the same market sector. SS also did not have any competition successes worthy of note, however this new car, the first to bear the Jaguar name, was a far more serious rival. William Lyons, the owner of SS cars was a brilliant designer from the same mould as Kimber, he also made all the major decisions, which meant that the Jaguar SS went straight into production, unlike the floundering Nuffield group which took until early 1936 to decide on the specification and

supply the parts for the SA. Initial publicity for the SA was forgotten by the time the car went into production some six months later. This delay was due also to Abingdon trying to uprate the specification to improve its standing against the Jaguar. The car initially had a 2062 cc engine and this was increased to 2288 cc to match the Jaguars 2663 cc unit. Normally this sort of alteration to the specification would have taken a matter of days when Abingdon were dealing direct with suppliers and were doing their own design work. It took months for the Morris engines division to change the

specification, as they saw it as a relatively unimportant job. Many impatient and disillusioned customers, over 500 in all, who had been waiting for their cars, changed their orders to the Jaguar SS which was ready for immediate delivery.

Last minute changes were implemented to take stock of the "opposition" which included the replacement of the original bolt-on wheels with centrelock wire wheels but even once production had started in earnest there were continual changes in specification which made a mockery of the so-called Nuffield efficiency. These changes could only be attributed to faulty initial design of the components, eventually even the complete chassis frame was modified. By the time of the 1936 Motor Show circumstances dictated a price rise with the saloon now costing £389 and the Charlesworth open tourer at £385. The Tickford Coupé was introduced at £415. Early in 1937 the engine capacity was changed yet again to 2322 cc probably to comply with Nuffield standardisation of models and there was little if any improvement in performance as a result. The performance could be described as adequate rather than exhilarating, with the car weighing in at almost a ton and a half and with only 75.3 bhp available, acceleration could only compare to its 18/80 forerunners. The SA did however have a genuine top speed of nearly 85 mph and could sustain a cruising speed all day long of 70 mph plus.

The SA Tickford Coupe featured is the car that was originally prepared for display at the 1936 Motor Show bearing chassis number 0502 and is believed to be the oldest known survivor of this model. The first 500 cars produced were all saloons and a total of 2738 cars were built between 1936 and 1939, it is not known how many of these were in fact Tickfords. The Tickford conversion allows for the hood to be folded back halfway or it can be wound down to the fully open position by means of a winding mechanism at the rear nearside of the car.

# SA
# Tickford Coupe

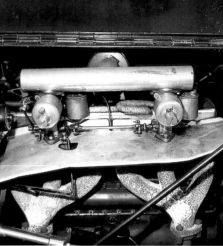

## SPECIFICATION

Engine Type: Water cooled in line
Number of cylinders: 6
Bore and Stroke: Early; 69mm x102mm Late; 69.5mm x 102mm
Capacity: Early; 2288 cc. Late; 2322 cc
Valve operation: Pushrod overhead valve
Compression ratio: approx 6.5:1
Carburation: Twin direct downdraught horizontal SUs
Power output: 75.3 bhp @ 4,300 rpm
Clutch: Wet cork
Gearbox: Manual 4 speed crash box on early cars. part synchro on later cars
Chassis: Twin sidemembers with cross members
Wheelbase: 10'3"
Track: 4'5⅝" front and rear
Suspension: Front: half elliptic springs with beam axle. Rear; half elliptic springs, live axle
Brakes: Lockheed hydraulic front and rear with 12" drums
Performance: Maximum speed: 85 mph
Fuel consumption: approx 17 mpg
Price new 1936: £415
Number Built: 2738 (includes saloon, open tourer and Tickford)

# VA 1.5 Litre Saloon

The MG Car Company was plunged into turmoil early in 1935 when William Morris sold MG to Morris Motors which formed the major part of the Nuffield Organisation. The organisation was primarily set up to rationalise Morris's sprawling business concerns and in the interests better efficiency allied to cost savings. Now known by the title of Lord Nuffield, it was well known that he personally disliked motor sport and it was in this area particularly that MG suffered most. Morris's new managing director, Leonard Lord was charged with streamlining the Nuffield empire and it was he who Cecil Kimber now became answerable. At a stroke MG's racing programme was cut midway through the 1935 season in the interests of reducing costs and this came as a severe blow to Kimber who up until then had virtually a free hand in development of racing vehicles and the everyday road cars. With the acquisition by Morris, Kimber was instructed to return far higher profits and the new management installed by Morris were solely interested in profitability related to simplicity and commonality of parts throughout the Nuffield range. With these new directives the Wolseley range of overhead camshaft engines ceased which immediately spelt the end for the MG PA/PB models and the Magnette. Kimbers biggest shock in all this reorganisation was the closure of the Abingdon design office with an enforced move by the team to the Morris design office at Cowley. H.N. Charles, Kimber's chief designer, now resident at Cowley was promptly put to task on the design of a new range of MG models, the first of which was to be the beginning of the T series, the TA Midget, which was launched at the latter end of 1935.

The model that really caused a stir, both in the motoring press and amongst enthusiasts was the all-new Two Litre model designated the SA Type. Launched in October 1935 it was a completely different breed of MG and was regarded by many as a belated successor to the 18/80 series which had ended production nearly four years previously. It was certainly a large car by MG standards, weighing in at over 30 cwts and exceeding 16 feet in length, nonetheless it had graceful lines and had to compete with other similar offerings from rival manufacturers such as the Jaguar SS 2.5 litre

saloon. Due to production delays caused mainly by inflexibility within the Nuffield group the MG saloon was at least six months in the making and as a result the impact of the initial launch publicity was totally lost. There were many dissatisfied customers waiting for their cars and a lot of them deserted MG in favour of the Jaguar. There were many production changes along the way in a bid by Abingdon to keep up with the competition and as a result of supply problems of components within the Nuffield group. Purists could not come to terms with this luxury MG conveyance due to its sheer size allied to pedestrian performance. It was undoubtably a quality vehicle however, which was refined and elegant and found its own niche in the market due to its extremely competitive price of £375.

More disdain amongst the purist was evident on the launch of the smaller stablemate the VA or one and a half litre as it became known. Introduced in time for the 1936 Motor Show, primarily as a replacement for the N type Magnette, it looked like a scaled down version of the SA. In keeping with the SA the new car was available as a saloon, an open tourer or as a coachbuilt Tickford convertible and they were priced at £325, £280 and £335 respectively. The VA was a neat well proportioned car and was distinguishable from its larger brother by the front nearside wingmounted spare wheel. Built on a conventional and sturdy MG chassis that was unique to the VA, the car had

a 9' 0" wheelbase and was 14' 3" long. The main chassis side members were of box channel construction and swept up at the rear over the rear axle line to accommodate a softer rear

suspension arrangement and to allow greater vertical wheel movement. Although the chassis was unique to the VA, other components such as the front and rear axles were shared with the Morris 12/4 and Wolseley 12/48. Lockheed hydraulic brakes with 10" drums were fitted to the VA unlike its predecessor the N type Magnette that had a cable operated system .

The power unit was a pushrod overhead valve type of 1548 cc and was common, with slight variation in the TA Midget, the Wolseley 12/48 and the Morris 12/4. The VA version had twin semi-downdraught SU carburettors and a bore and stroke of 69.5 mm x 102 mm with a power output of 54 bhp @ 4,500 rpm. The weight of the car, nearly 23 cwts precluded any meaningful performance, but nonetheless the MG was no slow coach with the saloon and convertible returning a top speed of over 75 mph and the tourer managing nearly 82 mph with the windscreen folded down flat. Transfer of power to the road wheels was via a cork clutch running in oil through a Nuffield four speed gearbox to a spiral bevel rear axle. A neat remote gear change was standard on the VA and it was the first time in an MG saloon that a part synchromesh gearbox had been employed. Sadly the VA suffered the same fate as the SA in as much as it took at least six months to get the car into full production after its official launch and it also suffered many component specification changes through its production life. The cork/oil clutch was changed for a dry plate variety, the carburettors, shock absorbers, road springs, rear axle casing, steering box and even the door handles were changed. In the engine department the camshaft was altered twice and white metalled big end shells gave way to bearings. It seemed that nearly all the components that comprised the VA were at some time either modified or changed which made life very difficult on the production line for the Abingdon workers. Despite all the interruptions the car did sell well during its two year production run with a total of 2,407 all variants leaving the factory gates prior to the outbreak of war. The 4 door saloon sold particularly well at £325 and had such refinements as a Bluemel adjustable steering wheel and Luvax dashboard damper control. There was also an option of the Smiths Jackall built-in hydraulic jacking system. The superb 1939 VA saloon featured belongs to Richard and Jacqueline Jenkins.

# VA SALOON

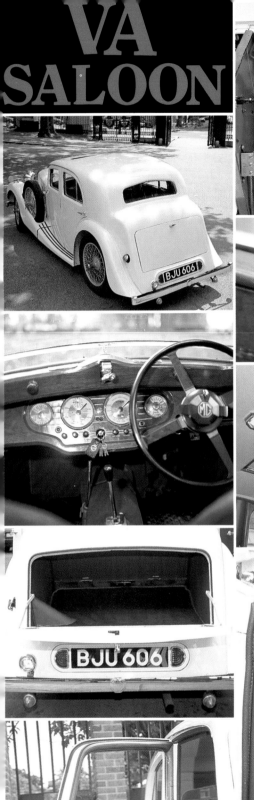

## SPECIFICATION

Engine Number of cylinders: 4.
Capacity: 1,549 cc.
Bore & Stroke: 69.5mm x 102mm.
Valve Gear: Overhead valves operated by pushrods.
Carburation:
Twin semi-downdraught SU HV5.
RAC rating: 12 hp.
Max Power: 54 bhp @ 4,500 rpm.
Transmission
Gearbox: 4 speed manual with synchro-mesh on 3rd and top.
Clutch: Initially single plate cork in oil, later single dry plate. Final Drive: Spiral bevel rigid axle.
Brakes: Lockheed hydraulic 10" drums all round.
Suspension: Semi elliptic front and rear with anti-roll shackles.
Hydraulic adjustable shock absorbers.
Wheels & Tyres: 5.00 x 19" centre lock wire spoke.
Wheelbase: 9'0".
Length: 14'3".
Width: 5'2".
Number built: 1,259 (saloon).

# VA Tourer

In 1935 Lord Nuffield sold the MG Car Company to Morris Motors and it was this rationalisation that lost MG its autonomy. The public image of MG was changed completely with the absorbtion of both MG and Wolseley into the Morris fold. When MG was under private ownership Cecil Kimber had a virtually free reign both with the everyday road cars and also with racing development work. With the acquisition by Morris, Kimber was instructed to return far higher profits and as a result the racing programme was ceased with immediate effect. He was also informed that production of the Wolseley based overhead camshaft engines was to stop which spelt the end of the PA, PB and Magnette models. Probably the biggest shock to Kimber was that the MG design office at Abingdon was to close with all new design to be transferred to Cowley. The new management installed by Morris were solely interested in profitability related to simplicity and uniformity of parts amongst the whole range of vehicles. This new policy ensured that the new MG models would be far less specialised than before with many interchangeable parts from other cars. This in turn would simplify servicing procedures and problems and allow longer production runs ensuring development costs would be recovered. Kimbers chief designer H. N Charles was promptly moved to the Morris design office at Cowley and embarked on a new range of MG models, the first of which was to be the launch car of the T series, the TA Midget that appeared at the latter end of 1935. This was followed by the 2 litre SA sports saloon and was a completely different breed to previous MGs. This car could be regarded as a belated successor to the 18/80 and was certainly a large car by MG standards. It was announced very soon after the launch of the Jaguar SS 2.5 litre but due to production problems lost its place in the market to Jaguar.

The 1. 5 litre VA was the third new MG to be introduced in 1936. The car strongly resembled a smaller version of the SA and likewise the car was available as a saloon, a tourer or Tickford convertible. The saloon was particularly neat in appearance and was distinguish-

able from the SA by its front wing mounted spare wheel. The chassis was of conventional MG design and was unique to the VA model with its 9' 0" wheelbase. The main side members swept up and over the rear axle line to accommodate a softer rear suspension arrangement and to allow greater wheel movement. The main members were of box channel construction, but at the rear additional strength was gained from lattice work box sections. Tubular cross bracing linked the front and rear suspension pivot points and there were additional supports for the transmission provided by longitudinal pressed members. Although the chassis was unique to the VA, other components such as the front and rear axles were shared with the Morris 12/4 and Wolseley 12/48 cars. Of course, the MG sported centre lock Rudge Whitworth wire spoke wheels, whilst the Morris and Wolseley had standard pressed steel disc type wheels. Lockheed hydraulic brakes. utilising 10 inch drums were introduced on the VA, moving away from the cable operated system used on its predecessor, the N type Magnette.

The engine used was a four cylinder pushrod overhead valve type of 1548 cc and was shared in different forms by the TA Midget (1292cc), the Wolseley 12/48 and the Morris

12/4. The VA version had twin semi-downdraught SU carburettors and a bore and stroke of 69.5mm x 1 02mm, the end result being 54 bhp at 4500 rpm. The weight of the car precluded any meaningful performance but nonetheless it was still no slouch with the saloon and convertible having a top speed of over 75mph and the tourer returning over 80 mph with the windscreen folded flat. Transfer of power to the wheels was via a cork clutch running in oil through a Nuffield four speed gearbox (synchromesh on third and fourth) to a spiral bevel rear axle. A remote gear change was standard on the VA and incidentally this was the first MG saloon to employ a part synchromesh gearbox.

Leonard Lord, Morris's abrasive managing director, made a policy decision to promote MG as the top of the range vehicle with Morris being the mass produced affordable version closely followed by the Wolseley variant as more up market. The idea was to make the MGs look that much better, faster and more exclusive and this they certainly were. The three versions of the VA were well priced against the competition with the 4 seat open tourer selling for £280 and the very smart drophead coupe at £351. The 4 door saloon sold for £325 and possessed such refinements as a Bluemel adjustable steering wheel and Luvax dashboard damper control. A Smith's Jackall built-in hydraulic jacking system could also be specified. The VA did sell well during its fairly short production life of just over two years, with a total of 2,407 being made before the outbreak of the war. The Morris installed management just could not sort themselves out during this period and the VA suffered as a result with many changes in the specification throughout its life. These continual changes must have made planned production a nightmare, such alterations included: dry plate clutch replacing the cork one, two crankshaft changes, changes to the steering, camshaft, carburettors, shock absorbers, door handles, road springs and so it went on.

It was never intended that the SVW range of MGs would be sports cars in the usual MG tradition, many of the purists were upset at the time, simply because these cars were a departure from their sporty predecessors. It was a deliberate attempt by the company to resurrect the earlier image as producers of refined, comfortable and well equipped high speed tourers. This was no doubt achieved and reflected in the sales figures, with a total of 2,738 SAs, 2,407 VAs and 369 WAs being produced.

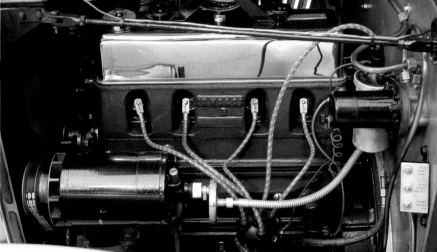

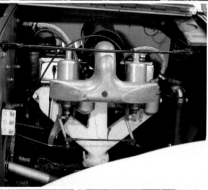

## SPECIFICATION

**Engine**
Number of cylinders: 4
Capacity: 1,548 cc
Bore & Stroke: 69mm x 102mm
Valve Gear: Overhead valves operated by enclosed pushrods.
RAC rating 12 hp
Carburation: Twin semi downdraught SUs
Max power: 54 bhp @ 4,500 rpm
Maximum speed: 81.82 mph
Acceleration: 0-50 mph; 14.2 secs

**Transmission**
Gearbox: 4 speed manual with synchromesh on 3rd and top only.
Clutch: Initially single plate cork insert running in oil, single plate dry clutch on later cars.
Final drive: Spiral bevel, rigid axle
Brakes: Lockheed hydraulic 10″ drums all round
Suspension: Semi elliptic front and rear with anti roll shackles. Hydraulic adjustable shock absorbers.
Wheels & tyres: 5.00 x 19″ Centre lock wire spoke
Wheelbase: 9′0″
Length: 14′3″
Width: 5′2″
Weight: 23cwt
Numbers produced: 2407 (591 tourers, 564 Tickfords, 2 open chassis, 1259 saloon)
Price new in 1937: £285 including jacking system

# TA Midget

In 1935, Nuffield sold the MG Car Company to Morris Motors and it was this rationalisation that lost MG its autonomy. Cecil Kimber was instructed that Abingdon was to return far higher profits and as a result the racing programme ceased with immediate effect. He was also informed that production of the Wolseley based overhead cam engines was to stop as part of the rationalisation programme which meant that building of the PA/PB and Magnette models would end. Probably the biggest shock to him would be that the MG design office was to close with all design work transferred to Cowley. The new management was solely interested in profitability related to simplicity and uniformity of parts and it was amongst many harassing restrictions that the new Midget evolved in the latter half of 1935. This new car was the first of the T series and the TA, as it was to become known, was not a car that Kimber and the workforce initially enthused about, their loss of independence and the loss of the very popular overhead cam engines causing much heartache.

The TA was to be the first of a line of T series MG cars that spanned two eras of pre and postwar motoring. There were to be five models in all; TA, TB, TC TD and TF and they were the last of the traditional MG sports cars. Announced in 1936 the MG TA Midget heralded cries of anguish from the purists who resented the fact that the overhead cam engine was to give way to a Morris 10 derived, overhead valve pushrod engine. The new TA was longer and wider than its predecessor, the P type Midget, the car was also much more comfortable and roomier and had the luxury of hydraulic brakes. It was also very competitively priced at £222 and represented very good value for money. The quality and straightforward design soon won over the stalwart overhead camshaft brigade as the TA had kept all the most desirable features and the larger engine provided much more pulling power throughout the range. This ensured that the car held its own in competition and the roomier body and improved and more comprehensive weather equipment made the car altogether a more exciting prospect for touring.

A traditional chassis was employed and although new, was of the familiar Abingdon design. The car was 8.5" longer than its predecessor the PB, which allowed more room in the passenger compartment, and the wheelbase was now 7'10" as opposed to the 7'3" of the PB. The main side members looked essentially straight from both elevations apart from the swept front end to clear the axle cross bracing was effected by four tubular steel sections and like its predecessors the chassis underslung the rear axle. At the front the chassis section between the new rubber engine mountings and the gearbox braces was boxed in. This had the effect of stiffening the side members where the torsional stresses were at their greatest because the rubber mounted engine now provided less rigidity than in the PB. Suspension was similar to the PB with half elliptic leaf springs at the front and rear with the rear ones mounted on Silentbloc bushes and sliding trunnions. The PB used friction damping at the front and hydraulic lever arm damping at the rear, but the TA was to use Luvax lever arm dampers all round. Cam gear steering was retained but a new feature was the fitting of Lockheed hydraulic brakes. The drums were considerably smaller than those on the PB and were reduced from 12" to 9" and

the fly-off type handbrake was to be retained as a standard feature. Spindly 19" outside-laced wire wheels shod with 4.50 section tyres had centre lock fixings. The two seater body was of traditional construction built on an ash wooden frame, secured to the chassis rails by 10 bolts. P type rear wings were employed and a vertical slat radiator replaced the earlier honeycomb type. A slab type 15 gallon fuel tank and spare wheel carrier adorned the rear end. The tank had a three gallon reserve compartment and this was operated by a dual petrol line from the tank leading to a dashboard mounted valve switch.

The new Midgets engine performed well in comparison to the earlier overhead cam engines that needed plenty of hard revving to gain the performance. The MPJG engine as it was coded used a 102mm stroke and a small bore of 63.5mm with a displacement of 1292cc derived from the Morris 10 engine. The horsepower rating was 10, which was all important for motor taxation and pricing in those days and engines with long stroke and small bore could attain reasonable power and performance without a rating penalty. Due to the Nuffield rationalisation plans all engines were produced from their Coventry engine factory with MG being built alongside Wolseley and Morris variants. The MPJG was rated variously between 45 and 50bhp at 4800rpm and had the benefit of twin SU carburettors, improved manifolding and camshaft. The power was fairly well down in the rev range, which when combined with the weighty flywheel and fairly high back axle ratio meant that the car would cruise comfortably without the drama associated with the high revving P types. The engine did have some rather innovative features with a belt driven cooling fan and pump together with a thermostat, instead of the dated thermosyphon method of cooling. The engine also consumed its own fumes to a limited degree with a pipe breather into the air cleaners from the valve cover and there was also a pipe from the crankcase that vented into the airstream under the car. The TA was certainly a lot cleaner and less pungent with fumes than its predecessors. The engine compartment consisted of a long flat centre-hinged bonnet and each half of the bonnet had a louvred side panel that itself was hinged to the top panel. This hinging arrangement allowed the panels to fold against each other and gave good access to the engine. On the nearside there was a 'power bulge' in the side panel to accommodate the dynamo. Tool boxes were thoughtfully built onto the bulkhead in true sporting tradition and twin six volt batteries were mounted beneath the rear luggage floor that was removable for access to the batteries and rear axle.

The water pump and associated 12" cooling fan were driven by a belt that also ran the dynamo which was mounted in a horizontal position alongside the engine rather than vertically mounted at the front of the engine as on the overhead camshaft cars. Other benefits included coil ignition, a distributor and 14mm sparking plugs and a welcome thought was the fitting of the oil filler cap into the top of the rocker box cover instead of deep inside the engine compartment. A huge 11 pint aluminium ribbed sump aided engine cooling and also contained a floating suction pump that rode on the surface of the oil thus avoiding the sludge that invariably built up in the bottom of the sump. The choice of gearbox was limited with the PB and Magnette boxes due to be phased out at

the same time as the overhead camshaft engines. There was only the Nuffield gearbox that was normally mated to the 102mm stroke engine to choose from. This meant that a cork faced clutch running in oil had to be utilised and this transferred the power via a non-synchromesh 4 speed box and high ratio bevel gear rear axle to the road wheels. The lack of synchromesh was no great disadvantage as no previous MG had ever been fitted with it but at a later stage TAs were to be fitted with synchromesh on third and top gear. A remote control gearchange was developed and close ratio gears were employed.

This Midget was probably the most civilised so far with the interior appointments good and designed with a degree of comfort in mind. The wider body gave the occupants more elbow room and the seats had separate cushions with a common back rest that was adjustable for rake. The hood and sidescreens were quite civilised with mica celluloid windows and the folding front screen was fitted with Triplex safety glass, quite a luxury for such a moderately priced car. The dashboard was symmetrically pleasing with large 5" speedometer and matching rev counter which carried an eight day electric clock and there was a central cluster with switches and ammeter etc neatly mounted. All the instruments were illuminated from the rear which proved very handy for night rallying and there was a map reading light on the passenger side of the dash with 30mph warning light looking very similar to the map light mounted in front of the driver. The spoked steering wheel was adjustable for rake and to complete the package, both driver and passenger had map pockets and outside door handles.

The TA was only available as a two-seater, unlike many of its predecessors and the car remained virtually unchanged throughout its production life, 3,003 cars were produced and they were almost identical apart from a few notable exceptions. They were the competition cars known as the 'Cream Crackers' and the delightful and rare Tickford drophead coupé together with the beautiful Airline fixed head coupe. Despite early misgivings about the TA, the car was a success story and sold well with little or no effective competition from such companies as Singer and Riley. The TA gave way to the TB which was launched in May 1939 and sported an all new engine which was to become renowned and designated XPAG. The 1939 MG TA featured is owned by Tony Newbold.

171

# TA

The M.G. Car Company Ltd.

## SPECIFICATION

Engine: 4 Cylinder.
Bore/Stroke: 63.5mm x 102mm.
Capacity: 1292cc.
Compression ratio: 7.5:1.
Valve operation: overhead valve operated by pushrod and rockers.
Carburation: twin semi downdraught SUs.
Power output: approx 50bhp @ 4,500rpm.
Clutch & Gearbox: wet cork, manual 4 speed non-synchro gearbox (early cars) 4 speed part synchro (late cars).
Rear Axle: Spiral bevel gears.
Suspension: Beam front axle with half elliptic springs and Luvax hydraulic lever arm dampers. Live rear axle, with half elliptic springs and Luvax hydraulic lever arm dampers.
Wheels: Centre lock wire spoke.
Tyres: 4.50-19" on 2.5" rims.
Brakes: Lockheed hydraulic 9" drum front and rear.
Wheelbase: 7'10".
Track: 3'9" front and rear .
Number produced (standard TA) 3003 between 1936 and 1939.
Basic price new of standard TA: £222. Tickford Coupe £269.
Performance: Max speed: 79mph. 0-50mph: 15.4 secs. Standing quarter mile: 22.8 secs. MPG: approx 30.

# TA Tickford Midget

The TA was the first of a line of T series MG cars that spanned two eras of pre and post war motoring. There were to be five models in all: TA, TB, TC, TD and TF and they were the last of the traditional MG sports cars. The TA was launched in 1936 to cries of anguish from the diehard MG enthusiasts who resented the fact that the overhead camshaft engine was to give way to a Morris 10 derived, overhead valve, pushrod engine. The new TA was longer and wider than its predecessor the P type Midget, it was also much more comfortable and roomier and had the luxury of hydraulic brakes. The TA very soon won over the purists as the TA had kept a lot of the earlier and more desirable MG features and with the bigger engine providing much more pulling power throughout its range, the car faired extremely well in competitions. This together with a far roomier body and more comprehensive weather equipment made the car altogether a more exciting prospect for touring. Competitively priced at £222, the car represented very good value for money with its straightforward design and quality it soon found its niche in the market place.

A totally new chassis of conventional MG design was employed and was 8.5" longer than its predecessor the PB. This allowed more room in the passenger compartment both lengthways and widthways with an increased wheelbase from 7'3" to 7'10". The main side members of the chassis looked essentially straight from both elevations apart from the swept front end to clear the axle. Cross bracing was effected by four tubular steel sections and like its predecessor the chassis underslung the rear axle. At the front the chassis section between the new rubber engine mountings and the gearbox braces was boxed in. This had the effect of strengthening the side members where the torsional stresses were at their greatest because the rubber mounted engine provided less rigidity than in the solid mounted PB engine. Suspension was similar to that of the PB with half elliptic leaf springs at the front and rear with the rear ones mounted on Silentbloc bushes and sliding trunnions. The PB used friction damping at the front and hydraulic lever arm at the rear, but the TA was to use Luvax dampers all round. Cam gear steering was retained but a new innovation was the fitting of Lockheed hydraulic braking instead of the cable operated type. Cecil Kimber never really trusted hydraulic brakes even though they had been around since 1921! The new brakes although smaller in diameter than on the PB, with wide shoes gave an equivalent braking surface area which was more than adequate for the standard performance of the car.

The new Midget sported a totally new power train, new that is to the MG fraternity but not new to the Nuffield organisation. In keeping with Nuffield policy of parts rationalisation and commonality there were many similarities with Morris and Wolseley power trains of previous years. Derived from the Morris 10 engine the MPJG engine as it was to become known in MG form, had a stroke of 102mm and a small bore of 63.5mm and displacement of 1292cc. The horsepower rating was 10 which was all important for motor taxation and pricing in those days whereby engines with long stroke and small bore could attain reasonable power and performance without incurring a rating penalty. The TA engine performed well in comparison to the earlier overhead camshaft engines that needed plenty of hard revving to gain performance. The MPJG engine was rated variously between 45 and 50 bhp at 4,800 rpm and had the benefit of twin SU carburettors, improved manifolding and uprated camshaft. The power was fairly well down in the rev range, which when combined with the weighty flywheel and fairly high back axle ratio meant that the car would cruise comfortably without the drama associated with the high revving P types. The engine carried some rather innovative features with a belt driven cooling fan and pump together with a thermostat, instead of the rather outdated thermosyphon method of cooling. The engine also consumed its own fumes to a limited degree with a pipe breather into the air cleaners from the valve cover and there was also a pipe from the crankcase that vented into the airstream under the car. This made the TA a lot cleaner and less pungent with fumes than its predecessors.

The TA Midget was probably the most civilised so far with good interior appointments that had been designed with a degree of comfort in mind. The wider body gave the occupants more elbow room and the seats had separate cushions with a common backrest that was adjustable for rake. The hood and sidescreens were a great improvement with mica celluloid windows and the folding front screen was fitted with Triplex safety glass, quite a luxury for such a moderately priced car. The dashboard was symmetrically pleasing with a large 5" speedometer and matching rev counter which carried an eight day electric clock. There was a central cluster with switches and ammeter etc neatly mounted and all the instruments were illuminated from the rear, a map reading light completed the package. The spoked steering wheel was adjustable for rake and the traditional flyoff handbrake was mounted to the left of the remote gear lever which operated the 4 speed non-synchromesh Nuffield gearbox.

The TA was only available in two seater form, unlike many of its predecessors and the car remained virtually unchanged throughout its short production life. 3,003 examples were produced and they were almost identical apart from a couple of notable exceptions. When the 1939 MG model range was announced in August of 1938 an additional body style for the TA was described. This was the delightful (and now very rare) Tickford Drophead Coupé. An earlier Airline fixed head coupe was produced privately by Allingham and sadly only one or two of these beautiful cars were ever produced selling at £295 they were extremely expensive compared to the standard model. The Tickford, although a factory approved and promoted body style, was not built at Abingdon, but at the Tickford Coachworks at Newport Pagnell from factory supplied partially completed TA chassis and bodies. Simply the entire body 'tub' which included doors, windscreen and pillars, rear quarter and folding hood were all new, although the front wings, running boards, radiator, rear wings and fuel tank were all from the standard car. The doors were not cutaway at arm height but were continued through from

front to rear at bonnet top height and they were to include wind down door windows and a front window channel that butted up to the front windscreen pillar. The screen itself was of far more substantial construction and carried painted instead of chromed side rails, the frame was rigid and could not be folded down, however the window could be hinged forward for added forced ventilation. It was intended that the Tickford should give the best of both worlds with open and closed motoring an option. The well padded hood sported toggle irons like those on the earlier larger MG convertibles and it certainly looked impressive on this far smaller car. The hood could be opened into the Coupé de Ville position just behind the drivers head and strapping it to the hood support bar. In this position and with the side windows fully wound up the occupants were not subjected to any wind buffeting unlike that experienced in conventional soft top cars with the hood down. The fold down hood did not disappear completely when in the fully open position and this meant that it did not look quite so smart as the normal TA when used in this way.

The interior of the Tickford carried some lavish appointments and could be more likened to a saloon, with the already mentioned wind up windows and wider doors, solid spoke steering wheel that could be adjusted for reach and rake. Additional improvements included direction trafficators concealed in the side scuttle panels and individual bucket type seats for the occupants. The obtrusive wiper motor found on the standard TA was now mounted out of sight with the wipers pivoted at the base of the screen instead of at the top. Very few TA Tickfords were produced which is not surprising considering the short time the TA model was left in production after the announcement of this body option. Another factor was no doubt the price for at £269 10s this raised the standard price of £222 by £47 10s and in those days this would have been quite a considerable amount. The beautiful TA Tickford Coupé featured forms part of a magnificent collection of MGs owned by John Shute.

# TA Tickford

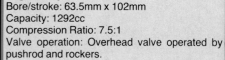

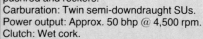

SPECIFICATION:
Engine: 4 cylinder in line.
Bore/stroke: 63.5mm x 102mm
Capacity: 1292cc
Compression Ratio: 7.5:1
Valve operation: Overhead valve operated by pushrod and rockers.
Carburation: Twin semi-downdraught SUs.
Power output: Approx. 50 bhp @ 4,500 rpm.
Clutch: Wet cork.
Gearbox: Manual 4 speed non-synchromesh (early cars) 4 speed part synchromesh (late cars).
Rear Axle: Spiral bevel gears.
Suspension: Beam front axle with half elliptic springs and Luvax hydraulic lever arm dampers. Live rear axle, with half elliptic springs and Luvax lever arm dampers.
Wheels: Centre lock wire spoke.
Tyres: 4.50-19″ on 2.5″ rims
Brakes: Lockheed Hydraulic 9″ drum front and rear.
Wheelbase: 7′10″
Track: 3′9″ front and rear.
Number produced: (standard TA) 3,003 between 1936 and 1939.
Basic price new: Standard TA £222. Tickford Coupe £269.
Performance: Max speed: 79 mph. 0-50 mph; 15.4 secs. Standing quarter mile; 22.8 secs. MPG: approx 30.

# TA Midget 'Cream Cracker'

'Mudplugging' or hillclimbing as it is more commonly known became an outlet for enthusiastic MG owners and works sponsored teams after the withdrawal of MG from serious motor racing in mid 1935. This decision came as a shock to a lot of the Company's customers also the workforce of Abingdon. There is no doubt that Cecil Kimber was totally against this policy set by Lord Nuffield and he sought other ways of supporting MG Owners in their indulgence of Motor Sport. He persuaded Nuffield to allow some record breaking attempts by Goldie Gardner in EX 135 and factory support of private individuals wishing to race or enter trials with their MGs. This did not involve financial support in any way and was more along the lines of assistance with the supply of specialist parts at reasonable prices, together with full technical advice.

The trials were directly descended from those of the 1920's whereby the organisers looked for the muddiest, steepest, rockiest and most tortuous tracks that they could find, sending highly modified cars from the bottom to the top in the shortest possible time. These climbs were generally on private property and sometimes involved travelling on public roads to another section of the trial. The cars were carefully scrutinized over each section and would incur penalty points or time penalties for leaving the set course or for slipping backwards on an incline. High performance was not absolutely necessary, but good traction was and passengers were compulsory if not essential to perform all sorts of contortions to assist in the forward progress of the car. On trials involving several climbs the passenger was put to work with navigating as well and in some ways was far more taxed than the driver! Sometimes competitors had to negotiate greasy gradients of 1 in 3 no less and there was a constant danger of cars tipping over sideways or in some cases flipping over backwards.

As a spectator sport mudplugging was very popular because the hillsides offered generally unobstructed views of the whole climb and the battles between MGs, Singers, Triumphs and Fords provided a real spectacle. It was against this background that many one marque teams were formed and most of them were nicknamed with some very obscure titles such as Tailwaggers, Grasshoppers etc. These names were signwritten on the bonnets of other marques, but the most famous and successful of the MG teams went under the names of Cream Crackers and Three Musketeers in England and The Highlanders and Blue Bustards in Scotland. In fact the first and probably the most well known of all the MG teams was the Cream Crackers formed in 1934. This was a private enterprise with the drivers of Maurice Toulmin, J. A. Macdermid and Jack Bostock all running PA type Midgets with enormous success. They were painted in the MG Car Company standard livery of Brown and Cream and all three won many events especially during 1935 when the team dominated the trials and were virtually unbeatable. The other team, known as the Three Musketeers had proved successful in NE Magnettes and works sponsorship was fairly evident, however towards the end of 1935 the MG Car Company were becoming more cautious with their support for trials cars and the Magnettes were sold off. The teams were re-organised and the Cream Crackers were supplied with new PB type Midgets which were

supercharged and with another year of successes behind them in 1936 the sponsored teams were looking forward to greater things in the following year. The overhead camshaft MGs were now out of production and were abandoned in favour of the new and more powerful TA Midget. They looked standard apart from the distinctive livery and with full works backing, the cars became very specialised.

The 1292cc engine was virtually standard on the 1937 model except for the raised compression ratio from 6.5:1 to 7.5:1 and Wolseley gear ratios were employed in the gearbox giving a far lower bottom gear. The bodies were standard apart from aluminium alloy panels and bonnets, together with lightweight cycle type mudguards. The cars were fitted with large knobbly tyres all round to aid traction and they also carried two spare road going tyres mounted on the fuel tank giving added weight over the rear driving wheels. Compressed air cylinders were carried in the rear compartment behind the seats together with heavy tools etc. to gain every advantage. The air cylinders were carried to speed the pumping up of tyres for using the car on public roads between different stages. Rear tyres would normally run as low as 10 psi when negotiating the slopes. The suspension arrangements were basically standard but the ground clearance height was raised to compensate for low tyre pressures at the rear and to give additional clearance for the sump at the front, uprated shock absorbers were fitted out of necessity. The original alloy sump was later replaced by the Wolseley pressed steel type because in spite of increased clearance the sumps were regularly damaged. This had disadvantages in that the oil did get rather hot at times without the added cooling effect of the original alloy sump and there was a distinct weight penalty by using the heavier steel variety. This was negated however by the fact that weighty sump guards were not needed unlike those employed by competitors.

There is no doubt that the sweeping successes of the Cream Crackers team sent sales of the TA Midget soaring and justified the factory involvement. It was the extensive publicity that

these events gained in all the motoring press which boosted the sales. The reports gave very good comparisons between all the different competing models and with MG coming out on top week by week. There is no doubt that these glowing testimonials sold the cars better than any carefully orchestrated advertising campaign. By the end of 1937 the competition from other marques was becoming quite intense and some highly modified cars were appearing on the climbs. The Austin Sevens for example had their suspension raised to amazing heights and the V8 Allards were managing to get the enormous power that they had on reserve into meaningful traction at the wheels. This all meant that the TAs had to be modified still further in order to retain their dominating lead over the competition. The engines were bored out to 1708cc and the MG gearbox was refitted which was able to withstand the increased power. Finally the front suspension was raised even further and very stiff Luvax shock absorbers were fitted. This made the ride most uncomfortable but did not deter the team from winning the championship again that year.

1937 saw the last full programme of trials, particularly for MGs. There were several factors that contributed to this, the main one being the introduction of more stringent regulations introduced by the RAC Motor Sport Administration. There were strong complaints by the general public over the mess and congestion that appeared on the roads surrounding the trials. This brought a ban on the use of knobbly competition tyres and surprisingly this made the works TAs quite uncompetitive affecting their traction far more than on some of the competitors cars. MG were unable to justify any further expenditure on developing a new improved trials car with the threat of war looming. Sadly the Cream Crackers were disbanded, however the private entrants under the Musketeers banner carried on competing right up to the outbreak of war with reasonable success amongst reduced entries due to the ban on the competition tyres.

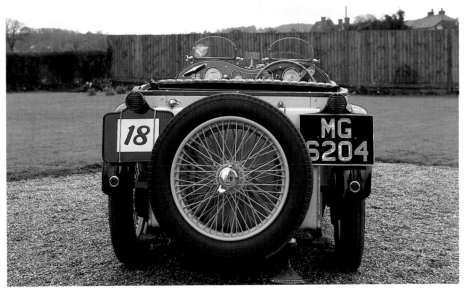

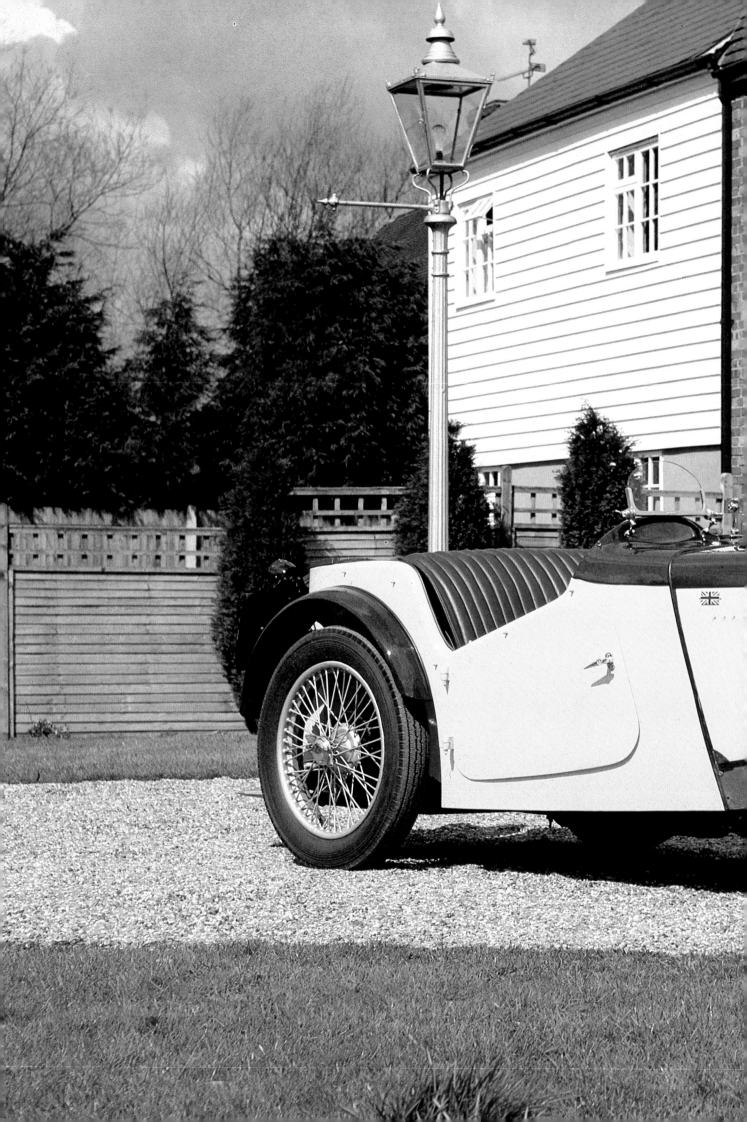

# TA

## 'Cream Cracker'

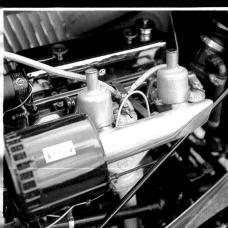

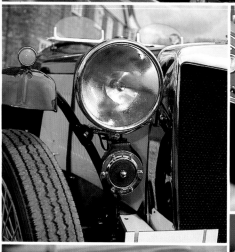

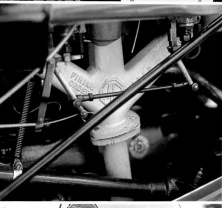

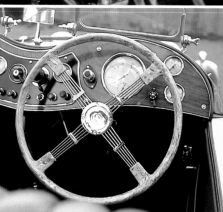

**Specification:**
Engine: 4 Cylinder
Bore/stroke: 63.5mm x 102mm
Capacity: 1292cc
Compression ratio: 7.5:1
Valve operation: overhead valve operated by pushrod and rockers
Carburation: twin semi downdraught SU's
Power output: approx 50 bhp at 4,500 rpm
Clutch & Gearbox: wet cork, manual 4 speed part synchro Wolseley gearbox.
Rear Axle: Spiral bevel gears 4.875:1 ratio
Suspension: Beam front axle with half elliptic springs and Luvax hydraulic lever arm dampers. Live rear axle, with half elliptic springs and Luvax hydraulic lever arm dampers.
Wheels: Centre lock wire spoke.
Tyres: 4.50-19'' on 2.5'' rims
Brakes: Lockheed hydraulic 9'' drum front and rear.
Wheelbase: 7' 10''
Tack: 3' 9'' front and rear
Number produced (standard TA): 3003 between 1936 and 1939.
(Cream Cracker TA 1292cc): 3
(Cream Cracker TA 1708cc): 3
Basic price new of standard TA: £222.

# WA 2.6 Litre Saloon

Following on from the success of the SA and VA saloons, the WA, announced in 1938 at the Motor Show, was to be the largest saloon yet produced by Abingdon. The car was similar in shape to the SA with quite stunning coachwork, however the interior was much more luxuriously appointed and there was more power available from the modified SA power unit. To understand the reasons for the introduction of this beautiful limousine we must go back to early 1935 and the revolution that swept through Abingdon. At this time not only was the racing programme curtailed but the amalgamation of MG with Morris and Wolseley was to have far reaching effects. Leonard Lord was appointed as the new Managing Director of the MG Car Company when Nuffield sold the concern to Morris Motors in July 1935. Cecil Kimber was retained at Abingdon but there was very little that he could do without the consent of Lord. Initially Lord said that he did not want to introduce any more MG sports cars as they interfered with his plans to streamline the organisation. Kimber however managed to retain some influence over the decisions and he did muster enough support to eventually change Lord's mind.

The end result of this conflict between Lord and Kimber was the introduction of the two litre SA Saloon in October 1935. Lord favoured this model as it was to be aimed at the lucrative luxury sports saloon market. This car was very closely based on the Wolseley Super Six and it was considerably bigger than any other MG previously produced. The idea behind this model was that it would enhance the company image and move away from the stark and somewhat basic sports cars that had made MG famous. The MG purists were a little dismayed with this new offering from Abingdon as gone was the familiar MG chassis to be replaced with a heavy conventional box-section Wolseley based variety. Also gone was the trusty overhead camshaft engine to be substituted with the Wolseley based Super Six two litre pushrod operated unit. With all this rationalisation of parts, Lord thought that all that was necessary to sell a Wolseley at an inflated price was to put an MG radiator shell on it and wait for the queue of buyers. Kimber and his supporters were soon able to dispel this theory and in the end he was given dispensation from Lord to design a new MG body for the Wolseley chassis. This he did with great success as evidenced by the very attractive and well proportioned body of the SA, although the car did suffer from the very inefficiencies that Lord was trying to eradicate with numerous component changes in order to take advantage of the standard items utilised by Wolseley. Ultimately the car did lose a lot of sales to the rival Jaguar SS due to delays in production once the model had been launched.

In 1936 the MG VA was introduced and this strongly resembled a scaled down version of the SA and was likewise available as a Saloon, Tourer or Tickford convertible. The saloon was

particulary smart in appearance and was distinguishable from the SA by its front wing mounted spare wheel. The VA or one and a half litre model as it was known was powered by a 1548cc four cylinder engine and had a wheelbase of 9' 0" and a track of 4' 9". Unfortunately it took just as long as the SA to put into production and likewise it suffered many production changes throughout its life. The VA however was a particular favourite with Cecil Kimber and he considered it one of the best looking cars that he had been associated with. His own personal VA saloon was modified and was fitted with a bored-out 1703cc engine that also powered some special VAs that were engaged on Police duties.

It could be assumed that MG had taken the large saloon concept far enough with the SA and VA models and had departed from the sports car image sufficiently (except for the TA Midget) to satisfy this sector of the market, however in the summer of 1938 the saloon car range was rounded off with the introduction of the WA or 2.6 litre saloon. This was an improved and larger engine SA that utilised a power unit not seen in any other Nuffield product of the time. There was an experimental version produced with a three and a half litre engine that was used in the top of the range Wolseley. This lorry based power unit however was found to be too heavy for the MG application and a modified SA engine was employed in the end. The WA

was undoubtedly the most luxurious MG ever to be produced by Abingdon and whilst superficially similar to the SA model, the body was far roomier and much better appointed. The comprehensive dashboard carried four smart octagonal instruments with a 100mph speedometer, revolution counter, water temperature, oil pressure, fuel gauge, ammeter and electric clock all incorporated in a neat oxidised silver surround. Immediately below this, neatly grouped around the ignition switch were rows of switches and warning lights for the other functions of wipers, lights, choke etc. The interior was very nicely finished with comfortable leather seats, leather door panels that sported beautifully inlaid wooden door cappings. Ventilation was well catered for with an opening front screen and individually opening quarter lights on the doors.

The chassis was similar to that of the SA, bearing the same wheelbase and front track, however the rear track was widened by more than three inches to improve the ride comfort in the rear. The brakes were improved by increasing the diameter from 12" to 14" and it was suggested by Kimber that the system would benefit from a Lockheed dual master cylinder due to the weight of the car. The power unit was derived from the SA engine and much was made of the fact that this was one of the first engines to employ a fully counter balanced crankshaft. The stroke of the engine remained the same at 102mm but the bore was increased from 69mm to 73mm giving a capacity of 2561cc. With a much higher compression ratio the engine then developed some 20bhp more than in VA form, but then due to the car weighing in more than 300lbs heavier than the VA all this extra power was needed to propel the hefty vehicle at acceptable speeds. Three types of coachwork were available on the WA chassis when it was announced in the summer of 1938. The saloon sold for £442, a Tickford drophead Coupé was available at £468 and Charlesworth Tourer could be secured for £450 but only nine of these were ever produced. Road tests by motoring journals of the day were very few and far between, but those that were published indicated that the WA gave very similar performance figures to those of the SA and VA. The acceleration was deemed unexciting when compared to the MG sports cars, however the WA was credited with a good top speed and the ability to maintain high cruising speeds at comparatively low engine revs. Other attributes were excellent roadholding, positive steering and efficient braking all very necessary considering the size and weight of the vehicle. With war looming over Europe the WA was ill timed and the wrong type of car to promote in the uncertainty of the future. As a result only 369 WAs were produced. Many purists of the time felt that the S, V, and W range of cars were unwieldy lumbering carriages that were unworthy of the marque, yet it was never intended that this range of cars should be sports cars in the true tradition of MG. It was a deliberate attempt by Abingdon to resurrect the earlier image as producers of refined comfortable and well equipped high speed tourers and whatever legacy these cars left behind them, there is no doubt that during the limited time that they were in production, they were very good sellers with a combined production figure for the S, V and W range amounting to 5,524 cars. The beautiful 1938 WA featured is owned by Peter Strawson.

# WA SALOON

## SPECIFICATION

Engine: In line water cooled.
Number of cylinders: 6
Capacity: 2,561cc
Bore & Stroke: 73mm x 102mm
Valve operation: Pushrod overhead valve.
Carburation: Twin semi-downdraught SUs.
Horse power (RAC rating): 19.82.
Power output: 95.5bhp @ 4,400rpm
Clutch: Dry plate.
Gearbox: Part synchromesh 4 speed manual.
Suspension: Half elliptic front and rear.
Wheels: Centre Lock wire spoke.
Brakes: Lockheed hydraulic. 14″ drums.
Wheelbase: 10′3″
Track: front: 4′5″
rear: 4′8.75″
Length: 15′11″
Weight: 24.25 cwts.
Number built: Late 1938 to late 1939: 369

Article and photographs by Richard Monk.

# TB Midget

Launched in May 1939, the TB did not look anything different from the TA and it was not until the bonnet was opened that the differences became apparent. However, there were some cosmetic changes externally, with the wire wheels now becoming centre laced as opposed to side laced on the TA and the semaphore type traffic indicators that were evident below the windscreen pillars on the TA were dropped on the two seater TBs but retained on the drophead coupes. The bonnet side panels had different sets of cooling louvres and the nearside panel sported a bulge to accommodate the large dynamo associated with the new XPAG engine. The hood had distinctive twin slots in the canvas forming the back windows, these however proved not to be very successful as the rearward vision was quite restricted.

It was during late 1938 and early 1939 that the XPAG engine was developed. It was a totally new engine with a fairly high state of tune and featured an enlarged cylinder bore of 66.5mm giving a capacity of 1250cc, which was down 42 cc on the TA engine. Despite this drop in capacity, the car ended up in the next taxation class going from to 10 to 11 horsepower. This was a direct result of increasing the bore and the car became a victim of the somewhat ridiculous horsepower formula. Making its first appearance in the TB, the XPAG engine would power almost every MG car and many special racing cars for the next 15 years and MG could not have foreseen that the engine would prove so successful, particularly with the Gardner MG that achieved over 200 mph. Phenomenal power outputs were achieved with the XPAG engine, particularly when supercharged and though it resembled the MPJG engine in as much as it was an overhead valve pushrod unit, that is where the similarity ended. The TB engine was altogether more appealing to the MG fraternity because it was capable of far more tuning than the old TA engine and was much more reliable into the bargain. Everything the TA engine lacked, the TB engine had in its favour. It had the larger bore of 66.5mm against 63.5mm and a shorter stroke of 90mm against 102mm, thus allowing faster and safer high revving. Maximum power was achieved at 5,250 rpm against 4,500 rpm of the MPJG unit and the output was a healthy 55 bhp. With the shorter stroke, there was some loss of torque but this was more than compensated for with a lower back axle ratio changed from 4.875:1 to 5.12:1. This extra power and higher rev limit ensured that there was no loss of speed at the top end of the range and the car performed well in the 55 to 70 mph area. The acceleration was marginally improved over the TA with a 0-60 mph time of 22.7 seconds which was nearly one second faster.

Because the XPAG engine had a stronger block, more efficient cylinder head and stronger counterbalanced crankshaft, the engine was far more receptive to tuning than its predecessor and with a far lighter flywheel the engine was altogether more responsive to accelerator movements. Developed from the Morris 10 engine the XPAG was specially produced to power the TB. The main new features that were introduced on the MG version were greater rigidity in all moving parts the already mentioned stronger block and crankshaft, short connecting rods with centre lengths less than four times the crankshaft radius, light alloy Aerolight pistons, shell bearings, larger

valves with the inlet being 10% bigger than the exhaust, large capacity oil sump with a full-flow filter system and finally a four branch manifold that fed into a Burgess straight through silencer system. An immediate recognition point under the bonnet was the repositioned air cleaner arrangement. This was horizontally mounted on the TA at the rear of the cast alloy inlet trunking, whereas on the TB it was now mounted transversely on a revised alloy inlet with its top end resting on the rocker cover.

The cooling system on the XPAG is worthy of mention because it was the design of the system that allowed the additional performance to be extracted from this now legendary engine. A rather ingenious flow system ensured that the block ran warmer than the cylinder head which was ideal for performance and also kept the mechanical wear down to a minimum at the bottom end of the engine. This is how the system worked; there were more than adequate water passages around the valve seats and the cooling water was directed particularly towards the cylinder head, through a pipe on the manifold side of the block and then to the back of the head. The water pump flow was therefore almost entirely channelled through the cylinder head, however there were water passages drilled through between the head and the block so that the block received mostly static water and it therefore ran at a slightly higher temperature. The original fan and thermostat system of cooling was retained from the MPJG engine with waterways introduced between the cylinder walls all of which aided mechanical efficiency.

A Borg and Beck dry plate clutch replaced the oil bath cork plate variety that had been commonplace on so many previous cars. There was also a new gearbox which was also employed on the VA saloon, with synchromesh on 2nd, 3rd and 4th instead of just the top two gears, but still in the same familiar casing. The gear ratios were also altered to cope with the lower rear axle ratio and these new ratios gave a road speed of nearly 16 mph per 1000 rpm which produced a very comfortable cruising speed of over 65 mph. An additional feature was the provision of a telescopic steering column which now became standard and was adopted from the TA drophead coupes as was the smaller capacity fuel tank now reduced to 13 gallons to accommodate the wider TB rear wings and slightly narrower body.

There was no doubt that the new engine and gearbox did wonders for the TB, making it so different from its predecessor, although the TA

was extremely popular with trials competitors because of its better torque characteristics and it was the TA that paved the way for the now legendary MG T series cars. The TB enjoyed a very short production life and when war broke out in September 1939 all MG production was brought to a rapid halt. In fact MGs model programme for 1940 was only announced after war had been declared and this meant that no sooner had the public been informed about the TB than they were unable to purchase one. In the four months of TB production only 379 cars were made. The Abingdon factory was cleared of all car components and was turned over to munitions work as soon as was humanly possible. Very soon aircraft pressed components, machine guns, overhauled tanks and army trucks were seen to be leaving through the factory gates instead of SAs, VAs, WAs, TAs and TBs. In 1941, Cecil Kimber secured a contract to make part of the Albemarle bomber aircraft, but this unfortunately was done without the prior knowledge and consent of the Nuffield board, which sadly resulted in the dismissal of Kimber. Tragically, Kimber was killed in a freak railway crash at Kings Cross station in February 1945 and without doubt MGs would not have enjoyed the respect and good reputation that the cars still enjoy to this day, without his enthusiasm and guidance. After 6 years of war, the Abingdon factory returned to sports car production under the leadership of a new director H A Ryder, who immediately struck up a good rapport with the slightly demoralised staff who were still reeling from the death of Kimber. It took just six months after the war ended for MG to come up with a replacement for the TB and even in the post war depression there was an anxious market looking for an improved version of the pre war cars. Hence the MG TC was born and in essence it was only a slightly revised TB with wider body and other minor modifications and improvements. The TC certainly looked the same with its general layout, styling, performance and handling almost identical to the TB, however this did not matter at all to the sports car buying public and the TC sold extremely well indeed and was billed as a post war sensation.

The 1939 TB featured is owned by Tony Newbold.

# TB

SPECIFICATION
Bore and stroke: 66.5mm x 90mm
Number of cylinders: 4
Capacity: 1250 cc
Horsepower: 10.97
Valve operation: Pushrod overhead valve
Power output: 54.4 bhp @ 5200 rpm
Clutch: Borg and Beck dry plate
Gearbox: Part synchromesh, 4 speed manual
Brakes: Lockheed hydraulic, 9″ drums
Suspension: Half elliptic front and rear with sliding trunnion and Luvax hydraulic lever arm dampers
Steering: Bishop Cam
Wheels: Centre lock wire spoke
Wheelbase: 7′10″
Length:11′7″
Track: 3′9″
Weight: 15.5 cwts
Max speed: 87 mph
Number built between early and late 1939: 379
Price new: £225 for the 2 seater. £270 for the Tickford coupe.

# Acknowledgements

My sincere thanks must go to the owners of the fine MGs portrayed within this book. Their patience is to be recognised whilst they spent seemingly endless time manoeuvring their car into position for the desired picture. I am also indebted to them for their help with information on the history of the vehicles and the loan of original brochures and period photographs is also acknowledged. Since the project started in *Enjoying MG* in January 1985, I am aware that some of the MGs featured have changed ownership, nonetheless I would like to thank the following members of the MG Owners' Club, MG Car Club and Octagon Car Club for their help, for without their willing co-operation, there would be no book.

Ian Hutchinson, Ron Gammons, Chris Barker, Rob Gill, Philip Bayne-Powell, Colin Tieche, Kevin Horwood, Barry Dean, Timothy Edwards, Barry Bone, William Opie, George Baxter, David Diplock, Terry Holden, George Ward, Peter Green, Peter Moores, Peter Gregory, Group Captain Wyndham Welch, Geoff Radford, David Naylor, Anthony Littlejohn, Robin Mace, Ron Saville, John Shute, Roger Thomas, Mark Warburton, Mark Sleep, Richard & Jacqueline Jenkins, Robin Lawton, Tony Newbold and Peter Strawson.

I must also record my appreciation to the British Motor Industry Heritage Trust for their permission to photograph "Old Number 1" and to Autocar for their kind permission to reproduce from original road tests of the era.

# Bibliography

The following books and periodicals were used as a source of reference:

*MG by McComb,* by Wilson McComb
*The MG Story,* by Anders Ditlev Clausager
*Magic of MG,* by Mike Allison
*Maintaining The Breed,* by John Thornley
*Early MG,* by Phil Jennings
*MG Past and Present,* by Rivers Fletcher
*The Art of Abingdon,* by John McLellan
*MG Sports Car,* by Autocar
*Great Marques,* by Chris Harvey
*The MG Magazine (1933-1935)*
*Autocar* (formerly *The Autocar*)